Interpenetrating waves of truth, resonating in a timelessness and universality of the Dharma, flow from the collected sayings of Jesus the Christ and Gotama the Buddha...

The Noble Eightfold Path of Christ

- Jesus teaches the Dharma of Buddhism

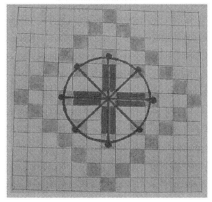

Thomas Ragland

National Library of Canada Cataloguing in Publication Data

Ragland, Thomas, 1962-
     The nobel eightfold path of Christ : Jesus teaches the dharma of Buddhism / Thomas Ragland.
ISBN 1-4120-0013-0
     1. Christianity and other religions--Buddhism. 2. Buddhism--Relations--Christianity. I. Title.
BT304.914.R33 2003   261.2'43   C2003-901247-6

TRAFFORD

This book was published *on-demand* in cooperation with Trafford Publishing.
On-demand publishing is a unique process and service of making a book available for retail sale to the public taking advantage of on-demand manufacturing and Internet marketing.
On-demand publishing includes promotions, retail sales, manufacturing, order fulfilment, accounting and collecting royalties on behalf of the author.

Suite 6E, 2333 Government St., Victoria, B.C. V8T 4P4, CANADA
Phone   250-383-6864   Toll-free   1-888-232-4444 (Canada & US)
Fax   250-383-6804   E-mail   sales@trafford.com
Web site   www.trafford.com   TRAFFORD PUBLISHING IS A DIVISION OF TRAFFORD HOLDINGS LTD.
Trafford Catalogue #03-0375   www.trafford.com/robots/03-0375.html

10   9   8   7   6   5   4   3

TABLE OF CONTENTS

CHRIST AND BUDDHA

The Christ:

In the face of the crowds Jesus went to the mountain. He sat surrounded by his disciples and spoke to them. [Matthew 5:1-2]

The Buddha:

When the recluse Gotama is teaching the Dharma to several hundred followers, at that time there is no sound, not a cough, not a clearing of one throat. All in that large assembly are poised in suspense of the Dharma that the Blessed One then teaches. [Mahasakuludayi Sutta 6]

Listen attentively to what these wise say. The words of Gotama and Jesus have been collected and preserved for a reason. They encapsulate the Dharma into pointers that are as relevant and practical today as they were 2000 years ago when the Christ taught them and 2500 years ago when the Buddha taught them. Humanity has collected sacred texts from ages past and from around the world. Two legendary figures from the collections of human written words come down to us as teachers of a higher caliber, believed to have been uniquely complete, surpassing the mundane.

The one called *Christ* is the inspiration for Christianity, the dominant religion of the West. He was known as Jesus, or more accurately, Yeshua. Among the titles given to this extraordinary human being are *Son of God, Messiah* (anointed), *Nazarene* (sacred), *Logos* (the Word), and *Savior of the World*.

The other called *Buddha* is the inspiration for Buddhism, the dominant religion of the Far East. He was known as Siddhartha Gotama Shakyamuni. This extraordinary human being was said to have become fully enlightened and to have taught the Way to becoming fully enlightened. The teachings he left behind for the enlightenment of the world are called the *Dharma*.

In eight steps the Buddha explained the *Way* for ordinary mundane unenlightened people to experience firsthand a transformation in their lives and purposes — *The Noble Eightfold Path*. As the Buddha lived to be 80 years old, quite a lot of his teachings were preserved. The focus of his teachings was to present the *Dharma* of his *Noble Eightfold Path*.

Separated by 500 years and 3000 miles, the Christ taught his message for the world. As the Christ only lived to be about 30 years old, according to Christian tradition, the teachings of Christ are limited to a handful of gospels. The focus of his teachings was to present the *Kingdom of Heaven*.

The *Kingdom of Heaven* as presented by the Christ is misunderstood if you think it refers to a place in the sky or something to come in the future. The *Kingdom,* for Christ, was a transformational force in the lives of those *born again,* redefining their world and their meaning and their relationship to what Christ called the *Father.*

To compare the teachings of the Buddha and the Christ, the differences in cultures and languages present walls, not only the differences in ancient India and Roman occupied Palestine, but the differences in the very accumulated histories of the Far East as compared to that of the Christian West. Add to this the elevated status of *one of a kind* that each is given within the religious traditions. We must press PAUSE, extract and abstract the words so that they can speak on their own merits. This is not an exercise for the narrow minded, or if you are insecure in your faith.

You can compare apples and oranges, no matter what you are told. But you have to adjust the rules, backing away from cold absolutes to make any progress at all. Terms must somehow be linked to represent near meaning—Sangha and Church, Dharma and Kingdom, Nirvana and Heaven. Any serious scholar will point out that these are not exact, but our purpose here is to link by purpose and by heart and by intent, to distill the very essence of what is being taught and let it then speak for itself.

It need not be explained that the teachings of the Buddha may be divided into eight groups, one for each of the stages of the *Noble Eightfold Path.* What is interesting is once we discover the resonances of thought from the teachings of the Christ, we now have the teachings of the Christ divided into these same eight categories.

Presented to you in written form is the Dharma as presented in agreement between the Buddha and the Christ. This should serve two purposes for the world. For one, Buddhists may be introduced to the Christ's teachings pretty much on their own terms. It may easily be noted that Christ echoed and amplified the Dharma of the Buddha. The other purpose is that Christians, who have spent lifetimes pondering the teachings of the Christ within the context of Jewish scriptures, may now easily note the agreements presented by the Buddha some 500 years before Christ. It is my hope that this will serve as material for building a bridge between the West and the Far East for some future ecumenical summit.

For now, I present into your hands—The Noble Eightfold Path of Christ.

Thomas Ragland

6th of November, 2002 AD

Percy Warner Park, Nashville TN

THE DHARMA

The words of the Buddha include the words of Lao Tsu from the Tao Te Ching and words attributed to the disciples of the Buddha – the Far Eastern school of thought.

The words of the Christ include the words of John the Baptist and words attributed to the disciples of the Christ – the Christian gospels school of thought. It will be left to each reader to contemplate Christ and to make any conclusions about his purpose in human history.

Where the teachings of the Christ go against the grain of traditional Christianity, there is an opportunity to reflect upon the vision and intent of how the Christ would have wanted Christianity to have developed. All are presented at face value, with no attempt to smooth over what the Christ appears to mean in order to make it more in line with traditional Christian thought.

The teachings of the Buddha represent Buddhism, define Buddhism, and in essence *are* Buddhism. The teachings of the Christ are overshadowed by the teachings of St. Paul and the fathers of the Church, and as such do not necessarily represent Christianity, define Christianity, or encapsulate Christianity as Christianity has turned out to be.

The central message of Jesus revolves around his parables describing what has been translated as *kingdom*. It is not an incorrect translation. The Greek word is *basileia*, and I'm presenting Greek using the alphabet that we can read since this book is not really for scholars anyway. *Basileia* means the extant of a realm of control. The *basileia* of a king's reign is the extant of the country. Thus, *kingdom* was the way that those working under the orders of King James back in 1611 translated this word. They got it right. They got it the best they could in English, detached by language and place and time from the Greek original, which was probably itself not the original language of the gospels. The word *basis* in English is actually derived from *basileia*. If we replace the word *kingdom* with the word *basis*, the message takes on a richer meaning. The teachings stop sounding like they are referring to some faraway kingdom in the clouds, some distant rule waiting on future events. The word *kingdom*, as applied to the teachings of Jesus, has the effect of detaching their messages from our present reality. We live in the kingdom of capitalism, in the realm of material possessions, on the street of day-to-day life. We can read the gospels over and over and as long as we think Jesus is talking about some pie-in-the-sky *kingdom* wanna be, then it has no relevance – pretty stories about sowing seeds and growing mustard and rising bread – la ti da. But if Jesus was instead talking about something that should and could be the very *basis* for our lives, then that changes things. It also changes the way we look at Jesus. That is how Buddhists look at the Dharma of the Buddha.

Christians for the most part look at the words of Paul as carrying the heavy doctrinal messages and the role of Jesus being to die and resurrect and do the *being Christ* bit. But what if the really heavy messages are contained in those funny sounding stories preserved as the teachings of Jesus? What if this *basis* that Jesus refers to is seen as the most important message that Jesus had to present to us? *Basileia*

3

also means a foundation, a purpose and mode for walking, the *being-in-control* of life, the extent of awareness. Your own personal *basileia* may be your cubicle at work, your car, your house, your family and friends, your realm of influence. What if you saw your realm of influence on a more spiritual level, as even being shared by others with the same spiritual goals, a *realm* that interpenetrated the hearts and lives of all who shared the same vision? What if you envisioned this realm, this basis, this influence as being worldwide in potential, breaking down cultural barriers, growing in the rich soils of various religious traditions and thriving on the diversity of applications? Call this basis the *Holy Spirit* and you begin to grasp at the power of the original Christian message. Call this basis *Dharma* and you have just opened up a channel to the East that brings in much light and explanation to what Jesus was saying. So to clarify the meaning of a Greek word being translated into English, I propose that we use an ancient Sanskrit (from India) word. *Dharma* has already been introduced as a word in itself to the English world. It is understood as implying a universal truth, an experienced holiness, a channel to the Divine, and an expectation of ethical responsibility.

As Josephus duly noted in his writings, you weren't allowed to write text back then that remotely sounded like you didn't fully support Caesar's rule. Do and die and have your words eternally burned. If you used *basileia*, you had to qualify it. Caesar ruled the Empire and no one had better talk about any other king or kingdom or basis for defining who you are politically. So the gospels followed this paranoia with always speaking of the *kingdom of God* or the *kingdom of heaven*. As long as they were talking about God or heaven then the Romans could dismiss it as pagan superstition.

This having been explained above, the following substitutions will be made in the transliterations. *Kingdom*, *Kingdom* of God, and *Kingdom* of Heaven will all be read as being *Dharma*. We can still divorce that Dharma from the Hindu and Buddhist concepts, at least initially. For Jesus presents his own Dharma, his own Eternal Truth, his own Way, his own Holy Spirit, and his own Inner Spring. What we can do, however, is to compare the Dharma as presented by the Christ with the Dharma as presented by the Buddha in a simple and open and honest fashion.

This Dharma of Jesus is a teaching to be followed and experienced. This teaching is a *pathway* to spiritual development. This teaching defines being a *Christian* in the eyes of Jesus. Note that this Dharma is not presented as a faith, not as a blind acceptance of grace, not as a magic bullet of atonement, not as a place to go to, and not an event to come. This Dharma is a lesson to be learned by each individual on a timeless and universal scale. This Dharma is a property of God that sanctifies those who come to experience it.

I claim a bit of poetic license to paraphrase translations to emphasize meanings and to simply understanding. I take the liberty of not only translating *basileia* as *Dharma*, but also by translating other individual words from the Greek gospels in accordance to their meaning in Greek. These differences in translations will be noted and explained in each case. All quotes from gospel and sutra are referenced so that the reader may go to any translation available to contemplate the intent of

4

what has been recorded. Concordances are available for those wishing to study the Greek, which require no specialized education or skills.

In short the Noble Eightfold Path can be understood as an eight-step program for self-directed spiritual development. Beginning with vision, we progress through defining what we treasure and what we leave behind. We concentrate on aligning our lives to this treasured vision, in our expression and communication, in our interactions and compassion, in how we present ourselves as being authentic and not sold out for money or status. Then we consider how we are to mature into being fruitful, harvesting from the positive effects that the Dharma has made in our lives. A direct connection to an inner light source, a deep inner well, is discovered. Ultimately we discover a detached holiness, perfection, and a rebirth. The Dharma comes as a tried and true experience, with observable and definable results. As Jesus said, we should judge the tree by its fruit. The Dharma is as valid for you as the results you get out of it. As it has been said, the Lord helps those that help themselves. You will get out of it exactly as much as you put into it.

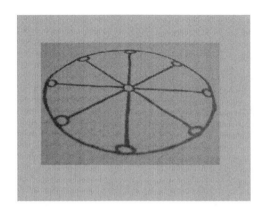

1. WHERE THE DHARMA GETS FIRED UP

It is wished upon the religions of the world by some that all paths somehow lead to the same destination. What both Christ and Buddha noted, however, is that you have to be able to distinguish the direct paths from the misleading ones. This is to say, you can get to the same destination from any starting point, but not every path from every point leads you on a direct way. Buddha taught that step one is to have the right view, which means that you have to know what are the wrong views. The right understanding is a vision that kindles the fire to be used as the fuel for the journey. What both Christ and Buddha agreed upon, from perspectives separated by age and culture, is that the Way is unconventional, uninstitutional, untraditional, uncontained. It is rather a personal provable transformation, a direct experience that binds a lasting change to the experiencer.

> The Dharma is not gained by calling me Lord, but by aligning yourself to the will of Heavenly Father. [Matthew 7:21]

Wow, did he really say this? The religion *of* Jesus is not gained by following a religion *about* Jesus. Belief without holiness, faith without works, is like being a fruitless leafless dead tree. The Way is a journey, not a destination. It is a means to salvation, not a magic bullet. The Dharma is about aligning with the will of God, resonating with that universal and eternal Truth that is somehow already known in the deepest part of our being.

It should go without having to be said that getting people to align with the will of the Father is the main purpose of Jesus having taught. This Dharma aligning *is* the message of Jesus for the world.

Distinguish right view from misleading views

> Better to have your own view, however small, than to live for another's view, however grand it may seem. [Bhagavad Gita 3:35]

The Dharma requires you to begin by having a view, a basis, a founding fire to fuel your decisions about life, to define your very purpose and destiny. It is a very important undertaking to adopt a view. If what you adopt as a view is that of a religion, of a church, of a minister, of an organization, or of a movement, you have forfeited your right to have a unique view of your own. You limit what can be known, what can be experienced, and what can be encountered. To control your own Dharma requires for you to be original and authentic and open to inspiration and intuition and mystical experiences. If you begin the journey by selling out your soul to an organized religion, you will probably miss out on a lot of potential for spiritual growth.

Luke 11:37-52 and Matthew 23:13-32 point *the four knots* at the teachers of religion—that they covet honor and respect, they mistreat people and persecute true prophets, they distort religion, and they bind people with their dogma. It is a universal and timeless unfortunate truth that organized religion often stands in the way more so than it helps those who are sincerely seeking spiritual growth. Trusting in organized religion can be like having yourself tied in knots. Anything that keeps you from realizing that *the real answers are found within yourself and experienced directly in your own life* is an obstacle.

Religion that is greedy for political control, for flaunting wealth, that persecutes those who are different, that judges by made up rules and unbendable dogma stands in the way of the Dharma. Number one on the Dharma path is *you have to see this truth.* As long as you think religion means going through some organized structure of authority, you cannot begin the Dharma path.

It is not to be taken as the point of these quotes that the Buddha was opposed to Hinduism or the Christ was opposed to Judaism. What they opposed was the mind control that comes with organized structured religion. What is really the point of their teachings is rather that when any religious group says that it contains and limits and controls truth, it is actually in the way of truth. It doesn't matter if the example given refers to Brahmins with their *Vedas*, or to rabbis with their *Torah*, or Christians with their *Bible*, or Muslims with their *Qur'an*, or even Buddhists with their *Ti Pitaka*.

Religion too often focuses on the useless details. Don't get caught in that trap. Religion that is fought over or used to divide people against each other is an obstacle to the Dharma.

Jesus used his mentor John as an example here. Consider who you think is the greatest spiritual teacher alive today with wise words and countless followers. Now consider what Jesus was saying in relationship to this great teacher. If you touch the Dharma within, you have found an even greater teacher. This is profound truth.

The Christ:

Alas for the teachers of religion (*nomos* – tradition, regulation, custom). They load unendurable burdens on the people and then they themselves do not help with the burdens. [Luke 11:4-6]

Alas for the teachers of the religion. They hold the key of knowledge away from the people. They do not partake and they prevent those who want to partake from having access. [Luke 11:52]

Keep your eyes open and be on your guard. Beware of the teachings of the Pharisees and Sadducees (Jewish holy teachers). [Matthew 16:5-12]

Leave the Pharisees alone. They are blind leading the blind. If you were blind could you guide another blind person? Wouldn't you both fall into a hole? [Luke 6:39, Matthew 15:14, Thomas 34]

You shut the door on the Dharma to keep people from finding it. You refuse to enter the door and stand in the way of those who wanted to enter. [Matthew 23:13]

Hypocritical Fundamentalists, you figure out exact tithing amounts for growing mint and dill and cumin. You neglect the very substance of religion—justice, mercy, and good faith. Forget the insignificant details and concentrate on what really matters. You are choking on gnats while you gulp down camels whole. [Matthew 23:23]

Off all born of women from Adam to John the Baptist, no one stands great enough to look John the Baptist in the eyes. I tell you that the least of you who becomes a child observing the Dharma is greater than John. [Thomas 46, Matthew 11:11, Luke 7:28]

The Buddha:

There are four things that will tie you in knots—the knot of covetousness, the knot of ill will, the knot of distorted understand of rules and vows, and the knot of adherence to dogmatic assertion of truth. Develop direct knowledge of these four knots with a full understanding of the need to utterly destroy them and abandon them. [Maggasamyutta 174]

Unskilled in this world and in the other world, unskilled in Mara's (devil's) realm and what is beyond Mara's realm, unskilled in Death's realm and what is beyond Death's realm, it can only lead to the harm and suffering for a long time for those who think they should listen to the Brahmins (Hindu holy teachers) and place faith in them. [Culagopalaka Sutta 3]

It is impossible for you to be sinking in the mud and to then pull out another person who is sinking in the mud. [Sallekha Sutta 16]

When the Brahmins learned in the three Vedas (Hindu Scriptures) teach a path that they do not know and have never seen, saying that this is the Only Way, they cannot possibly be correct. They are just as a line of blind men clinging onto one another, the first one sees nothing, the middle one sees nothing, and the last one sees nothing. They turn out to be laughable with their words empty and vain. [Tevijja Sutta 15]

Having generated such volitional formations, they tumble down the slope of birth, tumble down the slope of growing old, tumble down the slope of death, and tumble down the slope of sorrow, lamentation, pain, displeasure, and despair. [Saccasamyutta 42]

They are profound in that commitment to wrong and useless doctrines. Clinging tightly to them, they cannot let them go. [Lotus Sutra 2]

Don't judge a religion by its appearance

Don't let them pull the wool over your eyes. Not everyone who wants to appear as a holy person is on the path of the Dharma. Here is another shiny hook to stop your Dharma progress. Beware who you trust with identifying your Dharma progress with. Religions and religious people are often completely devoid of a Dharma filled heart. One easy to spot identification of religious people to avoid like the plague is when they tell you that you have to be exactly like them or burn forever in hell. Just shake your head and walk away.

You can't even trust those religious leaders that on the surface appear to be sincere and know what they are talking about. Examine thoroughly anyone who you place in the position of being an authoritative teacher in your life. Most people would gasp at the thought of selling their soul to the devil. What would it gain for you to have them promise you the world in exchange for your soul? Careful.

Don't just try to look the part of being holy. Don't just acknowledge as being holy those that look the part. Looks are deceptive. Consider as being beautiful and shiny the state of the heart being cleansed. Value the inner beauty in others and in yourself.

The Christ:

They will say to you — Look it is there, look it is here. Make no movement. Do not set out in pursuit of them. [Luke 17:23-24]

Beware of hypocritical holy men who come to you disguised as sheep but underneath the mask they are ravenous wolves. You can spot them by examining their fruit. [Matthew 7:15]

Where you hear that someone will reveal the Christ if you go to them, disbelieve it. False Christs and false prophets arise with wondrous signs and miracles, enough to deceive the elect. But this is not possible for I have warned you. [Matthew 24:23-25]

Whitewashed tombs look beautiful on the outside, but inside are filled with the rotting dead. From the outside those who appear to be holy may be full of hypocrisy and unhealthy desires. [Matthew 23:27-28]

Like cleaning the outside of a cup and leaving the extortion and intemperance to grow on the inside. The part of a cup that needs cleaning is the inside. [Matthew 23:25-26]

The Buddha:

What good is sheep's clothing? Inwardly mangled they manage to make their appearance shine. [Dhammapada 26:12]

Evil demons, that disguise themselves as "angels of lights" in the last age of this world, will be present everywhere in abundance. Some will tempt you openly with greed and lust. Others will pose as holy and learned masters. No one will escape their presence. Many will be lured into the swamps of defilement and thus lose the Path to Enlightenment. [Surangama Sutra: Importance of Keeping the Precepts]

In the End Times there will be false teachers who teach under the pretense of having authority, asserting that they have received their Dharma from a respected master, deceiving ignorant people. [Surangama Sutra: Importance of Keeping the Precepts]

A person is not easily known by external appearance. A first impression should not be trusted. Some move about in disguise. Inwardly they are impure. Outwardly they are beautiful. [Kosalasamyutta 11]

Like a beautiful bronze dish, new from the shop, clean and bright, with a dead body inside, loathing, repugnant, disgusting. [Anangana Sutta 29]

Search out right view

Personal choice to actually respond to the opportunity to cross over from the mundane ordinary mechanically reactionary life to the mystical inspired enlightened life is the beginning of the Dharma path. Dharma requires that you plug yourself in of your own free will.

11

Non-intellectual truth

Dharma is not about being intellectual. It is not about having gone to school. Words or institutions do not contain it. It is not purchased. It is available to anyone who wishes to begin the journey that is willing to stop trusting in the intellectual institutional definition of what it is to be religious.

The Christ:

The Blessed Father took the secrets of heaven and earth and hid them from the educated and respected, revealing them only to little children. [Luke 10:21, Matthew 11:25]

The Buddha:

They are learned and proud. I am detached and hard to reach. They are sensible and prudent. I am neglected as a deaf-mute. They have collected their wealth. I am simple and poor. In the eyes of man, I am Poor and simple, but I have the food of Mother Way to nourish me. [Tao Te Ching 20]

Letting go

Your own religious tradition background as received from your parents and culture may very well be the main thing holding you back from making progress in the Dharma. Letting go of religion may be the best thing you can do to spiritually advance. It sounds like a strange conclusion, but mystics from different ages and cultures have come up with the same thought. St. John of the Cross spoke of the dark night of the soul in which everything that used to be comforting has to be abandoned. Let it all go. It will be less to have to carry with you to argue about and keep you from considering ideas that don't coordinate with your dogma baggage. Erase it all and begin with a clean blank slate. Whatever is eternally of any value will be added back.

The Christ:

You can't partake of the new wine by putting it into old wineskins. The wine will burst the skins. You will spill the wine and destroy the skins. Supply fresh skins to partake of the new wine. [Mark 2:22, Matthew 9:17]

You can't enjoy new cloth by using it to patch old raggedy clothes. The patch will just shrink away and make the tear worse. [Matthew 9:16]

The Buddha:

Do not adhere to possessed views or hold them stubbornly. Let go of them easily. Practice effacement. [Sallekha Sutta 12]

Dharma is like a raft—useful for crossing over, then useless to hold onto. [Alagaddupama Sutta 13]

A blind man went to search for white beautiful spotless clean clothing. He was deceived into accepting a dirty soiled garment to wear. One day he regained his sight and with it the desire to continue to wear that dirty soiled garment was abandoned. He burned it, thinking about killing the man that tricked him and cheated him. [Magandiya Sutta 20-24]

Begin the journey

The fire needs to be perpetually fanned to keep it blazing. Ever present in potential, waiting for free spirits to blow upon its flame, the Dharma survives being snuffed out by institutions and books and rituals. The secret to Dharma being able to revive over and over throughout human history is that Dharma is a verb and not a noun. Like a song, it exists only when someone is singing it. The notes on the paper only preserve it as a potential song.

Child

A simple conservation of a calm dignity that doesn't dwell long on being upset or arguing about trivial matters, that sees all of that as being games for *grown ups* and getting in the way of life, is the entry point for the Dharma, the beginning of the journey. The being *born again*, being a child again, is the advice that Jesus is most remembered for.

Eiserchomai means more in Greek than *enter* in English. Eiserchomai is usually translated as enter. Its meaning in Greek is that of acquiring, mastering, fulfilling, reaching, resulting, coming to be among, accompanying, appearing with, growing into. It implies an accompanying of a presence, an active participation. Only *paidion* (immature, young) can *get it*. *Dechomai* means to receive, accept, and partake of. It takes the *paidion* to *dechomai* the Dharma and *eiserchomai* it. Without plugging the Dharma back into a mature intellectual paradigm of analysis, without cross referencing and checking against established tradition, without labeling or trying to justify, children simply try things and observe the results, being open to new experiences. Without such a childlike openness, the Dharma can never become a part of life.

The Dharma of Jesus was not an intellectual accomplishment of the old. In fact, it cannot be intellectually acquired. The Dharma is a game to be played and not a lesson to be learned.

The Christ:

Do not stop the children from coming. They are the keepers of the Dharma. [Luke 18:15-16]

Anyone who does not accept the Dharma as a little child shall never accompany it. [Thomas 22, Matthew 18:3-5, Mark 10:14-15, Luke 18:16-17]

A person that has seen many a day will rush to ask a seven-day-old baby about the place of Life. Then that person will discover Life. Many that think of themselves as being first will become last until they discover unity. Little nursing babies can look into the Dharma. [Thomas 4]

The Buddha:

A baby is weak of bones and muscles, but is spiritually pure. A child's unity is unbroken. To know the continuation of this unity and wholeness, you must return to the original state of simplicity. That which is fully-grown is in the process of decaying. [Tao Te Ching 55]

Realize the foolishness of angered response, keeping the mind *one* in tranquility with the simplicity of a child, conserving the spirit. [Tao Te Ching 28]

Preserving humility and the calm breathing of non-aggression, you become like a little child. [Tao Te Ching 10]

Purity

You can polish up your view, unclutter your mind, purify your heart, and brace yourself for a journey into a greater purpose.

The Christ:

Jesus put many cloths into a vat of dye and they all came out sparkling white and new. [Philip 63.25-30]

The Buddha:

A cloth that is defiled and stained becomes pure and bright with the help of clear water. [Vatthupama Sutta 12]

> If you start with a clean bright cloth and dip it into dye, the result will be beautiful. It is because of the purity of the cloth. When the mind is undefiled, a happy result may be expected. [Vatthupama Sutta 2]

Within

Wherever you are, you are now carrying with you all you need to touch the sacred. No need to find a temple or church. No need to order a book. It is wherever and whenever. Anything that is not valid from any perspective whatsoever is not the Dharma. As long as your heaven is out there somewhere, you are missing out.

The Dharma is within our grasp and not something that is going to come or going to happen. It is expressly not a distant place, up in the sky or elsewhere. It is expressly not something alien to us, but a part of us. It is like the Buddhist concept that we all have Buddha Nature within, it has been there all along, and we just need to awaken to realizing that it is there. It is not as if we have gotten lost as a displacement in space, but rather we have amnesia or ignorance that we have been home all along. It is about waking up. It is a resurrection that takes place in the soul, an experience, an acquaintance with eternity, and a shift to a higher level of thinking, a supernatural knowing of how it all fits together.

The Christ:

> Is the Dharma from up in the sky? Then birds have reached it first. Does the Dharma come up out of the earth (from the depths of the sea)? Then the fish have reached it first. The Dharma lives in our hearts and we have reached it first. [Thomas 113]

> The Dharma is not seen. You cannot find it here or there. In order to see the Dharma you have to look within each of us. [Luke 17:20-21]

The Buddha:

> The Great Way is spread out. It can be discovered at any location. [Tao Te Ching 34]

Gate keeper

You are the gatekeeper of your own life. You are wise, competent, and intelligent. You know what you need to get rid of in your life. You know what you need to partake of. If you put everything in your life through your inner *Christ gate* then your life will be shepherded and protected and long. Dharma is a protective filtering, a channeling of all ideas and reactions through the gatekeeper of *Buddha nature*, of *Christ consciousness*.

As you control the channel being watched on television, you can control the visions being presented to the eyes and your reaction to the visions. If you see Dharma then your world is filled with light and harmony and hope and purpose. If you see the waves crashing, the whirlpools spinning, and the sharks and sea serpents attacking, then your world becomes a dark and scary place. You control your perspective. You can dwell on the negative or you can stand on the high ground above the scary waters, putting it into its proper perspective.

The Christ:

I am the gate of the sheepfold. Anyone who enters through me will be safe. All who go in and out will find pasture. I am here so that they may live long lives. I am the good shepherd whose purpose is to protect the sheep. I am the good shepherd. I know mine and mine know me. The Father knows me and I know the Father. My purpose is to protect the sheep. [John 10:7-15]

If your vision is focused, your world will be filled with light. If your vision is scattered, your world will be filled with darkness. [Matthew 6:22-23]

The Buddha:

The gatekeeper posted is wise, competent, and intelligent. He keeps out strangers and admits acquaintances. While he patrols the walls, he doesn't allow holes large enough for cats to slip through. He is assured that all large creatures that enter or leave this city do so from the one gate. [Satipatthanasamyutta 12]

The Buddhas, the ones that the world venerates, desire to open the gateway to the Buddha's Dharma so that all sentient beings can achieve sanctification. This is why they appear in the world. [Lotus Sutra 2]

The eye is the ocean for a person. Forms are its currents. You who stand firm in the midst of the currents of forms are said to have transcended the ocean of the eye with its waves, whirlpools, sharks, and sea serpents. Crossed over, gone beyond, the Brahmin stands on high ground. [Salayatanasamyutta 228]

Revealing

The revelation of the Dharma is for nothing less than a perfect vision that shows a perfect practice that leads to deliverance — to Nirvana — to the Father. The only Path to the Father is this living revealing Way — the Noble Eightfold Path. Jesus so identified himself with this Dharma that he could proclaim that he was the only Way to the Father. But remember that we are talking about the religion *of* Jesus and not the religion *about* Jesus. His Dharma is the only Way. His Dharma is the *aletheia*, which is a Greek word meaning revealing, uncovered, visible. No more hidden secrets of initiation. The Dharma was plainly revealed and presented as the only Way that leads to the ultimate goal. Without journeying upon this Way, it was proclaimed, you will never ever arrive at the destination.

The Christ:

I am the way, the revealing (aletheia), and the life. You do not come to the Father except through me. [John 14:6]

The Buddha:

The liberated mind possesses three unsurpassable qualities—perfect vision, perfect practice of the way, and perfect deliverance. [Culasaccaka Sutta 26]

The Blessed One has attained Nirvana and he teaches the Dharma for attaining Nirvana. [Culasaccaka Sutta 26]

Training Yoke

For all that was said to avoid external teachers and learn from the Dharma within, the exceptions are noted that learning the Dharma from a fully enlightened master could only speed up the process. Thus we in this book turn to the sayings preserved that are attributed to both the Buddha and the Christ. If you take the Christ as your spiritual inspiration, you will find yourself advancing quickly in the Dharma. If you take the Buddha as your spiritual inspiration, you will find yourself advancing quickly in the Dharma. For nearly the first time in history, we now have the ability to take the Buddha and the Christ together and consider the inspiration of their agreements. This generation is truly blessed.

Mystics speak of praying without ceasing, of remaining in a state saturated with divine bliss. A joyful peaceful tranquil knowing of the Dharma is a living experience, a continuous drawing from the teachings of life itself. Life is the classroom, the tuition free.

The Christ:

Come to me all you overburdened with your concerns and I will give you rest. Put on my harness and let me train you. I will be gentle and soft hearted with you. You will find your own personal rest. Truly my harness is a comforting one, a light one to wear. Thomas 90, Matthew 11:28-30]

The Buddha:

In a delightful saturation of the Dharma of Buddha, the mendicant monk discovers supreme peace that transcends eternity with the supreme joy of Nirvana. [Dhammapada 25:22-23]

It may be understood how the entire holy life is good friendship, good companionship, and good comradeship. By relying upon me as a good friend, those subject to birth are freed from birth, those subject to aging are freed from aging, those subject to death are freed from death, and those subject to sorrow are freed from sorrow. It may be understood how the entire holy life is good friendship, good companionship, and good comradeship. [Maggasamyutta 2]

What is the heavy burden to have to carry? It is the craving that demands renewed existence, along with delight and lust. It is searching for delight here and there. It is craving for sensual pleasures, craving for existence, craving for extermination. This I call quite a heavy burden to have to carry. [Khandhasamyutta 22]

A thoroughbred colt gets used to wearing the bit, then the harness. Once the colt is peaceful in this, the trainer teaches him to keep in step, to run in a circle, to gallop, to charge, to display royal qualities in the heritage of a horse fit for a king. The fastest, most responsive, gentlest horse will be rewarded with rubbings and brushings. Hear the Dharma with eager ears. [Bhaddali Sutta 33]

You are not alone

Power of transformation

All sins will be forgiven. [Matthew 12:31]

No one is too evil to partake of the Dharma path. Everyone can start *now* and begin the journey. It has amazing transformational qualities that can set anyone on the right way. *Hamartema* is the Greek word for sin, which means to lose the game and thus to not win the prize, to miss out on the allotment, to fail at the craft. *Aphiemi* is the Greek word for forgiven here, which means forsaken, abandoned, left behind, omitted, given up, ignored.

> Failed attempts will be ignored for those who begin to try. [Matthew 12:31]

It is valid to translate it this way. What is not ignored by the Dharma is when you don't value the holy and don't even try. To consider that the prize of the Dharma is not worth the effort of working toward winning is the unforgivable sin, the losing of the game due to not trying. It is unforgiven, not because some external being is then forever angry, but because the person does not begin to try. To try and to fail is miles ahead of to not try at all.

The Christ:

> A man with a dirty spirit came out of the tombs toward Jesus. The man lived in the tombs and no one could control him, even with chains. He was often secured with fetters and chains, but he snapped the chains and broke the fetters. No one had the strength to control him. All night and day he wandered between the tombs and the mountains, howling and cutting himself with stones. Seeing Jesus from a distance he ran falling at his feet. [Mark 5:2-6]

> They came to Jesus seeing the demoniac sitting there properly dressed and in his full senses, and they were afraid. [Mark 5:15]

The Buddha:

> A murderous bloody violent merciless killer laid waste to villages, towns, and districts. He constantly murdered people and made a garland of their fingers. [Angulimala Sutta 2]

> The bandit walked as fast as he could but could not catch up with the Blessed One who was casually walking. He stopped and called out to the Blessed One—stop, recluse! Buddha answered—I have stopped. You stop too. [Angulimala Sutta 5]

> Suppose you were to see that bandit had shaved, dressed in a yellow robe, and entered the homeless life. He abstains from killing living beings, from taking, from lying, from eating at night, from sexual pursuits, virtuous and of good character. If you saw him like this, how would you treat him? [Angulimala Sutta 11]

> DHARMA LESSON: Every dharma that contradicts itself
> will not last. What I give is God's Dharma, which has been
> of such shock to you. [Matthew 12:25-28]

So many so-called answers, religions and philosophies and political frameworks, simply don't stand up to the wash. A dharma is a foundation for building, and shifting sands does not make a good platform for building a home. When holy books are analyzed and the contradictions are made evident, people lose faith in religions that are founded on the books. When traditions are replaced with scientifically provable conclusions that oppose such things as the earth being flat and the sun revolving around the earth, people lose faith in religions that are founded on ancient ways of thinking that are venerated and preserved. The *dharma* presented to Jesus was that his Dharma was alien to Jewish tradition and thus was an evil force. They taunted him with remarks that his attempt to cast out the demons was empowered by demons. His Dharma shocked their simple paradigm of there being a holy and inspired internal Jewish tradition of *good* and there being all of the other ignorant and misleading traditions of the pagan world outside of the Jewish framework of *evil*. His Dharma should be a shock to the simplistic paradigm of there being a holy and inspired internal Christian tradition of *good* and there being all of the other ignorant and misleading traditions of the pagan world outside of the Christian framework of *evil*. Fundamentalists of any genre look at their own self-contradictory scriptures as being holy and divinely inspired. They look at scriptures from any other culture as works of the devil, corrupting the simple minds of the chosen people. In xenophobic shock, those opposed to Jesus rejected the Dharma of Jesus because it contradicted their narrow vision of good and evil, of chosen and rejected, of blessed and damned, of Messiah vs. Rome.

The charge that Jesus, who was obviously trying to teach and heal and help, was using evil forces to fight evil, could only make sense if *evil* equates to *foreign*. In the Fundamentalist Christian mindset, foreign ideas are *pagan* and *of the devil*. Buddhist scriptures are thus tricks of the devil to beguile those who refuse to shun them. That Jesus was preaching Buddhist ethics in the framework of Jewish Law and *Pure Land* in the framework of heaven, and Buddha in the framework of Messiah, and Sangha in the framework of community, and Dharma in the framework of his own set of ethical teachings — is what they were calling an evil.

Living Dharma

> DHARMA LESSON: Heavenly Father, send us your
> Dharma that your will may be realized on earth as in
> heaven. [Matthew 6:10]

As the Dharma defines the heaven (kingdom) of God, the same Dharma defines the extent of heaven on earth. The Dharma is spread through the evident ethics of compassion, of peace, of a unity of all of us trying to make our own collective destinies better. For the Christ in each of us, we have this vision of a Dharma that exists only in our heaven — that place inside of us that shines as an inner light. For the Christ in each of us, our prayer is for there to become channels to share this with the day-to-day reality around us, to make our world a little bit better place, one encounter at a time, one smile at a time, one kind word at a time, one good deed at a time, one good intent at a time. It is through receiving the Dharma and channeling the Dharma though our lives that it is up to us to bring about heaven on earth. It is a large dream. It is the prayer of Jesus. It is his Dharma vision –

> Holy Father, cause Dharma to appear. Give us our daily bread. Forgive our mistakes. [Luke 11:2-3]

Kingdom (Dharma) *come*, is the English translation for the Greek word *eltho*, which means to accompany, to appear, to bring, to grow, to enter, to establish, to setup, to make evident. If there was one main wish of Jesus it was for this Dharma to be made evident in the lives of people. This is the real deal. No ancient texts. No mystical sounding prophesies of old. This was a Living Dharma to be nurtured and shared by caring hearts.

As somewhat of a magical amulet text that gives us the power to realize this prayer of Jesus, the following four key words are appended as the conclusion of the Lord's Prayer: basileia dunamis doxa aeon, for thine is the kingdom and the power and the glory forever. [Matthew 6:13] *Basileia* is Dharma, the basis and foundation and driving force behind being able to accomplish anything spiritual. It is that inner presence of Holy Spirit that guides us all into an interbeing of purpose and destiny. *Dunamis* means miraculous powers, the magic implied in linking to the Dharma. This magic moves mountains for us, takes a tiny seed and makes it grow, resonates synchronicities for us, gives us intuitive insight. *Doxa* is the underlying source of the Dharma, the glory and dignity of God. *Aeon* is perpetuity, an eternal substance to grasp while experiencing a transient fleeting life in a world of change and death. This magical formula is offered as a gift: Dharma with evident miraculous force from a source and of a nature that is eternal.

Forgiveness is a very central issue with Jesus. While the Essenes were trying to be pure in culture and the Pharisees were trying to be pure in the letter of the Law, and while the faithful journeyed to the Jerusalem Temple to sacrifice animals for forgiveness — Jesus is saying that his *dad* is quite prepared to simply overlook any shortcomings (sins) we may have. It was added to this thought that Christians are not only forgiven, they are expected to be forgiving. This is a very simple yet powerful prayer that solidified the position of Jesus as having a Father whose felt presence can feed us with a divinity that is our salvation.

Dharma king

The purpose of the Buddha and the Christ is to teach the Dharma to the world. The *bodhisattva vow* is the desire to teach the Dharma to every sentient living being on the planet. Dharma vision is not for a personal salvation, but is rather a dream for the world to partake of a sanctified state of mind — to keep the wheel turning.

The Christ:

Pilate — Are you the king of the Jews?

Christ — Mine is not a kingdom (Dharma) of this world. For this I originated. For this I came into this world — to teach the truth. All who belong to this truth will hear my voice. [John 18:33-37]

The Buddha:

Sela — Gotama, you should reign over all peoples as king of kings.

Buddha — I am already a king, Sela. I am supreme king of the Dharma. I rotate the Dharma wheel and no one can stop it from turning. [Sela Sutta 16-17]

2. WHERE THE DHARMA GETS INSPIRED

For the Buddha, the very next stage after contacting the right view is to develop right mindfulness. Mostly, you are what you think. You have to be inspired by something to be motivated to do anything at all. You are defined by what you will. One of the greatest realizations of the Dharma is that we have free will. For all of the predestination and karma preached by various religions, the Dharma's answer is quite simple. We have free will and can will a change in the very direction and purpose of our being at any time. Perhaps the chapter should be called *where the controls to the Way are placed in your hands*. Some of us when we are young imagine in dreams that our hands are wings and we are in control of the very flight of our lives. You are hereby invited to consider the birds in flight. [Matthew 6:26]

Focus

If you have sold your soul to having to make money to pay for the big house and bills from an expensively shopping family, the Dharma cannot take the precedence it deserves in your life. If the Dharma is your treasure, the focus of your mindfulness, it is your own personal duty to abandon whatever distracts you from living a life devoid of materialistic concerns. This is not saying you cannot have a family and own stuff. This is saying it is not a requirement in your life for you to be chained down to the slavery of spending all of your energy to make money. There is more to life than that. If you have a spouse and children that understand your values, then more power to you.

Heart defined by desires

You define yourself. You are known as the totality of what you stand for, what you represent, what you are after, what you value in life. Since you have defined yourself, you can always redefine yourself.

The Christ:

Where you find what your treasure—you define your heart. [Matthew 6:21]

The Buddha:

Whatever you frequently think of and ponder upon, that defines the inclination of your mind. [Dvedhavitakka Sutta 6]

It is impossible to engage in sensual pleasures without being enraptured by sensual desires that overwhelm the perceptions of thoughts. [Alagaddupama Sutta 9]

23

Follow my advice and have your pile of gold loaded on carts and dumped into a river. For on account of gold there arises for you sorrow, lamentation, pain, grief, and despair. [Ratthapala Sutta 22]

Elimination

You find yourself by giving up everything you have wrapped around yourself. Enlightenment is not about collecting ideas, but in the letting go of ideas, of attachments, of possessions, of identifications.

To be forced to choose between the Way and your own father, mother, wife, children, brothers, sisters, and even your own life, is a link in common between the disciples of Jesus and Gotama. [Luke 14:26] The concept of carrying your own staff [Luke 14:27], of being responsible for your own spiritual journey in the detachment from all that can stand in the way, is yet another common link.

Matthew 10:38 is such an amazing teaching of the Christ. It is usually translated as "take up your cross" which immediately gives the image of the Roman means of executing criminals. I don't think Jesus really preached that we should all be executed martyrs. Going back to retranslating the Greek, I am torn between two translations:

Anyone who doesn't *take his staff* and follow in my footsteps is not worthy of my concern. [Matthew 10:38]

Anyone who is not willing to *pull out his stake* and follow in my footsteps is not worthy of me. [Matthew 10:38]

The implication is the same, either way. We are called to leave behind the life that the world wants for us and take in hand the life that the Dharma calls us to.

It would be a better modern concept to say once you've jumped out of an airplane with a parachute, there is no looking back. Once you accelerate a racecar to 200 miles per hour and are approaching a curve, there is no looking back. Once you become disillusioned with the old religious traditions, the old weedy field that hasn't gotten you anywhere, and you decide to plough it up and plant crops and make some use out of the field, you are pretty much dedicated to the project once the oxen is walking and you have your hand on the plough. You are facing a renewal of life and purpose. The old weeds are being turned under. The dirt is being loosened and softened. The soil, the plot of land, the field — is the heart. One tiny mustard seed of Dharma planted in a ploughed heart (empty mind made ready for new concepts) will grow into a large shrub.

Throughout the towns and villages, preaching and proclaiming the good news of the Dharma [Luke 8:1] we encounter Jesus as a traveling mystical teacher. The Dharma that he presents is an encapsulated transmittable universal Truth, an oral tradition, a Shekinah (presence) of Divine Force, a Holy Breath that can be breathed by all who are born of this Dharma.

The Christ:

If you prefer father or mother to me, you are not worthy of my concern. If you prefer son or daughter to me, you are not worthy of my concern. If you are not willing to *pull out your stake* and follow in my footsteps, you are not worthy of my concern. You who strive to preserve your life will miss out. You who abandon your life for my sake will find eternal security. [Matthew 10:37-39, Matthew 16:24-25, Mark 8:34-35, Luke 9:23-24]

Leave behind the dead to bury their dead. Your duty is to go and spread the Dharma. Once the hand is on the plough, there is no looking back. This is the way of Dharma. [Luke 9:60-62, Matthew 8:22]

Without forsaking everything, you cannot be my disciple. [Luke 14:33]

The Buddha:

Nothing in this world is lasting. Don't think of possessions as being stones. Think of them like foamy bubbles, shimmering and then evaporating. You must learn to quickly let go of it all and go along your way. [Lotus Sutra 18]

He who is free from all attachment, he I say is a holy man. [Udanavarga 33:52]

In setting aside the intellect and the ego, the enlightened one finds freedom through detachment. [Aggi Vacchagotta Sutta 15]

I see bodhisattvas (saints) who have given their very lives, their work and their community standing, have left behind wives and children, and followed the ultimate Way. I see bodhisattvas who would gladly put their head on the line, their eyes, life and limb, in exchange for the Buddha's Dharma. [Lotus Sutra 1]

It is a gain to lose and a loss to gain. [Tao Te Ching 42]

Are you anxious about your mother and father? Are you anxious about your wife and children? Whether or not you are anxious, you will die anyway. So please abandon your anxiety. [Sotapattisamyutta 54]

Are you anxious about what pleasures you can sense as a human? Celestial pleasures sensed are more excellent and sublime. [Sotapattisamyutta 54]

As the mighty rivers reach the sea, they lose their former individuality and become parts of the great ocean, so do disciples forsake their former families and nationalities and become part of Buddha's family. [Cullavagga 9:1:4]

It is not easy to remain living at home and to lead the holy life utterly perfect and pure as a polished shell. Go forth from the home life into homelessness. Abandon your fortunes. Abandon your relatives. [Kandaraka Sutta 13]

Watch what you treasure

People are not remembered in history books because of the bottom line of their bank accounts. The Dharma is a secret treasure, invisible to those who don't know how to see it, but evident to those who measure their life's value by it. What is of any value ultimately is what effect you had on the world, who you helped, who you taught, who you guided, what you gave of yourself. The rest is left behind for relatives to fight over after your funeral. What you contributed to the world remains as your legacy.

Get over yourself. Get over being number one. Get over thinking that the sun should rise and set in your armpits. Get over resent, jealousy, envy, competition, and climbing that totem pole at work. Get over getting that promotion.

Concern about possessions is the greatest distraction from attention to the Dharma. People spend lifetimes collecting and protecting and paying for expensive homes and vehicles and toys. They stress themselves out in jobs they hate to pay the bills for everything that they were so convinced that they just couldn't live without.

Be careful not to sell out your soul to the pursuit of collecting impermanent decaying trinkets. Wealth is eternally valueless. You are eternally not identified with anything you collect in this life, not even your body. It will all have to be let go of. Nothing can cling to your spirit after the death of your body.

The Christ:

Sell your possessions and give charity to those in need. Do not stock up your earthly valuables. Moths and worms could destroy everything. Thieves could break in and steal everything. Stock up on your heavenly valuables. These moths and worms cannot destroy and thieves cannot break in and steal. Where you find what your treasure— you define your heart.   [Luke 12:33-34, Matthew 6:19-21]

Watch and be on your guard against the lure of any type of wealth.   Life is not made up of possessions. It cannot be purchased by collecting more than you need. [Luke 12:15]

If you wish to be complete, sell your possessions, giving it all to the poor to assure yourself of heavenly treasure. [Matthew 19:21]

A man walking through a field discovered a great treasure.   He hid the treasure in that field and went and sold all that he owned to purchase that field. [Thomas 109, Matthew 13:44]

I notice you pick the best place to sit. If a more distinguished person arrives, you will be asked to move in your embarrassment.   If you pick the worst place to sit, the host will ask you to move to a better seat. Everyone who puts himself first will be humbled. Everyone who humbles himself will be exalted. [Luke 14:7-11]

A certain rich man owned a lot of good land. He built huge barns to store his crops in and a large house to store his wealth in.   He thought to himself that he had everything he needed to live comfortably for many years.   Take it easy, eat, drink, and be merry, he would say.   But God answered him—Fool, tonight they are coming for your soul. Then who will own all of the wealth that he had accumulated?   He was rich with wealth but not rich with God. [Thomas 63, Luke 12:16-21]

James—My advice for the rich: start crying now, weep for the misery that is your destiny. Your wealthy treasures will rot, moths eat your clothes, and your precious metals corrode. The same fate awaits your body. It will corrode away. [James 5:1-3]

27

The Buddha:

If a workingman comes into possessing wealth, he will experience pain and grief in protecting it. How can he keep it from being taxed by the government, or stolen by thieves, or burned by fire, or washed away by flood, or stolen by relatives? He guards and protects, sorrows, grieves, laments, until finally he beats himself in distress saying he wishes he never had it. [Mahadukkhakklandha Sutta 10]

No one who owns a house, who doesn't abandon the fetter of concern for the house, on the death of the body has come to the state of having extinguished suffering. [Tevijjavacchagotta Sutta 11]

When your house is on fire, you salvage what you need, leaving the rest to become burnt. The world is on fire with aging and death. You must rescue by giving. What is given is what is salvaged. What is given produces good fruit. What is kept is not fruitful. It is taken by thieves and governments, lost in the fire and burnt. [Devatasamyutta 41]

Wisdom is the precious gem of humanity. Thieves cannot steal merit. [Devatasamyutta 51]

The perfect sage dresses in the cheap clothing of The Poor, but treasures The Way like a hidden gem. [Tao Te Ching 70]

If it is possible to forsake a limited pleasure and thus discover eternal happiness, the wise will abandon the limited pleasure seeking the eternal happiness. [Dhammapada 21:1]

The greedy do not make it to heaven, those fools who shun charity. The wise that give freely will find much happiness for eternity. [Dhammapada 13:11]

The wise man will act righteously, creating for himself a treasure that no one can steal, and that cannot rust away. [Khuddakapatha 8:9]

Which is more valuable—your soul or your wealth? You should seek that which you treasure, being very careful to treasure the right things. [Tao Te Ching 44]

To dress richly, to collect weapons, and to indulge in sensual excess and wealth, are just invitations to the robbers. [Tao Te Ching 53]

If the Perfect Sage wishes to convince people to abandon concerns over wealth, he should not himself value expensive items. [Tao Te Ching 3]

It is possible that a disciple may wish to get the best seat, the best water, and the best food in the house, instead of another disciple. It is possible that some other disciple ends up with the best seat, or the best water, or the best food in the house. The anger and the bitterness become like open sores. [Anangana Sutta 15]

It is possible that a disciple may wish to get the most beautiful robe, instead of another disciple. It is possible that some other disciple ends up with the most beautiful robe. The anger and the bitterness become like open sores. [Anangana Sutta 15]

I see wealthy men of this world in ignorance failing to share from their gathered wealth. Greedily they hoard their riches away, still trapped by longings for more sensual pleasures. [Ratthapala Sutta 42]

As he dies nothing can follow him, not child, not wife, not wealth, not royal estate. [Ratthapala Sutta 42]

Vangisa — Whatever exists here on earth occupying space, composed of form, part of the world — it is all impermanent, it all decays. You live as a sage once you have penetrated this truth. People are bound to their possessions — to what they can see and hear, sense and feel. Abandoning desire, unmoved, you are a sage who clings to nothing around yourself. [Vangisasamyutta 2]

You who take refuge in the Sangha and develop right views are truly not poor for yours is a life not lived in vain. [Sakkasamyutta 14]

If you have an underlying tendency toward something, then you are measured in accordance with it. If you are measured in accordance with something, then you are defined in terms of it. [Khandhasamyutta 36]

Though you possess hundreds of thousands of worldly possessions, you are still subject to death. All collections will be dispersed. All pile-ups will be thrown down. All assemblies will be taken apart. All life must end in death. [Udanavarga 1:21-22]

Value

Look out for the Dharma as your number one concern instead of focusing on worries and needs.

The Christ:

Martha is distracted by her worries about the outcome of so many concerns. Mary has discovered the only concern that is worthwhile, what is better, what can never go wrong. [Luke 10:41-42]

The Buddha:

The Blessed One left behind some food one evening. One disciple remembered the lesson to treasure the Dharma and not the material and passed by the food, remaining hungry and weak for the night and the following day. Another disciple ate the leftover food, being full for the night and the following day. The Blessed One commented: Blessed is the disciple who has passed by the food. He has learned the lesson of how to be satisfied with few concerns, contented, not selfish, easily maintained, and in control of his desires. Out of compassion for you I have taught you to be my heirs in the Dharma and not the material. [Dhammadayada Sutta 3]

Movement

Making a start

It is said that a journey of a thousand miles begins with a single step. You may not think that you could possibly matter. That one vote doesn't count for much. That contributing one-dollar to a charity won't go very far. But Dharma is magic. A small amount brings about a great change. It becomes an amazing force, aligning and synchronizing events and causing obstacles to fall away. And the impossible becomes history. Just add a small seed to the prepared soil and watch the plant grow. Just add a pinch of yeast to the dough and watch the loaf poof up into light and fluffy bread. Magic.

The field is the heart. The mustard seed is a brief encounter with the Dharma. It hides itself unseen at first just beneath the surface. It is so tiny that even if you were to dig about in the dirt, you might not find it there. It has a way of making a significant presence in the life of the heart that possesses its magic. Come back and look at that same field in years to come and witness this amazing mustard bush, with birds landing on it and singing. Come back and observe the life of one touched by the Dharma and witness the change and growth and purpose and interaction.

Yeast is the Dharma. The bread is the heart. When yeast is mixed with the flour, such a small amount is used that it goes unnoticed. These insignificant tiny specks of nothing have so much potential, however. The otherwise flat unleavened bread rises when baked into a light and fluffy loaf. It transforms the flour into something that it could not have achieved on its own.

All of the little hints of Jesus come together in a thread of brilliance. Worry as much as the lilies. Let tomorrow take care of itself. Life is more than food. The body is more than clothing. The son of man has nowhere to lay his head and rest.

When the *Christ* is seen as the food and drink, as the healing medicine for a spiritually sick world, as the robe of glory to be worn, the eternal mansion in the eternal kingdom, we could easily transpose these religious concepts to be referring to the *Buddha Nature* that is discovered within the practicing Buddhist. I will leave it up to each reader to consider drawing the same conclusion.

The Christ:

Dharma is like a tiny mustard seed that a man throws into his garden. It grows large enough for birds to sit in its branches. Dharma is like a pinch of yeast that a woman put into the flour that made the bread rise into a large loaf. [Luke 13:18-21, Matthew 13:31, Matthew 13:33]

The Buddha:

A tree that it takes both arms to encircle was once a tiny twig. [Tao Te Ching 64]

Be Careless

The Christ:

Set your hearts on the Dharma and all of your needs will be supplied. [Matthew 6:33]

Blessed are the Poor. In Spirit they own the Dharma. [Matthew 5:3]

Don't worry about how you're going to eat, about what you're going to wear. The birds of the sky don't work. They don't plant and harvest and store in barns. Still they eat. How much greater are you than birds? Can all the worry add a day to your short lifetime? Just one day—beyond your power—so why worry about small things? The flowers of the field don't work. They don't spin fibers or weave fabrics. Still they are dressed up finer than the richest king. If flowers that grow today and are dried and burned tomorrow have such clothing, how much more will you be taken care of? Don't worry about what you will eat or drink, letting it split your mind. The entire world worries about such. Your Father knows what you need. Set your heart on the Dharma and you will discover that all of these other things are supplied. Nothing to fear, Father is pleased to supply you with Dharma. So sell your possessions and give to the needy. Carry a purse that has a Treasure that will never be all spent, that cannot be stolen or destroyed. For what you treasure defines your very heart. [Luke 12:22-33]

The Buddha:

The Perfect Sage is disinterested in his own personal concerns, and thus they are taken care of. [Tao Te Ching 7]

Happiness is living without possessions among those who possess much. Happiness is living without ties. Happiness is living without struggling among those who strive anxiously. [Gandhari Dhammapada 167)

Clothing, bedding, food, drink, and medicine—none of these are worth worrying about. Instead concentrate upon what it takes to preach the Dharma and set your desires on completing the Way of the Buddha. [Lotus Sutra 14]

Who is content to be satisfied with what is at hand will avoid troubles and long endure. [Tao Te Ching 44]

Be contented and you are already rich. [Tao Te Ching 46]

Faith Seed

The Christ:

My daughter, be assured—your faith has made you healthy. [Matthew 9:22]

The Buddha:

If a person is completely free of all doubt and hesitation and from the depths of heart has an instance of faith, he will indeed be blessed. [Lotus Sutra 17]

Fragile faith

The Christ:

Anyone who brings down the faith of one of the children would be better off being thrown into the ocean with a large stone tied around his neck. [Mark 9:42, Matthew 18:5-7, Luke 17:1-2]

The Buddha:

If a bad person, completely lacking in goodness, should for an aeon stand before the Buddha and continuously curse and taunt him, that person's offense would be light compared to the person who speaks one harsh word to curse or belittle the disciple who reads and recites the Lotus Sutra. [Lotus Sutra 10]

If anyone should speak against those who uphold the Lotus Sutra, he will suffer greatly for this crime. [Lotus Sutra 20]

Love centered

DHARMA LESSON: What are the greatest commandments of religion? To love God and direct all of your feelings and rational thought and understanding and energy to that One Love, and then to love your neighbor as if they were all close family members. To appreciate that these are the greatest commandments bring you very near to the Dharma. [Mark 12:28-34]

The universal golden rule is the same in Jewish ethics as Buddhist ethics or Hindu ethics or Christian ethics. The example here is from Deuteronomy 6:4-5 and Leviticus 19:18, from the Jewish Torah. The same example could be found in nearly every human tradition in the world. Simple truth. Treat outsiders like they're family. There may be a limit to how far we extend this. It may reach to our next-door neighbors, in keeping a watch on their property and lending a hand as needed. It may extend to everyone that is part of the same culture. It may extend to a universal brotherhood of man. It may extend to all sentient life. Jesus grounds this in the making of a connection to the force that the Jews call God. The fourfold direction of energy toward that focal point is worth studying here. All of kardia (heart, feelings, will), all of psyche (soul, rational thinking), all of dianoia (mind, understanding), and all of ischus (strength, energy, force), are to be

33

focused upon the Divine, the result of which is the channeling of a force of love that extends to those let into your heart.

There is perhaps no better introduction to the Eightfold Path within the Jewish framework than this. Right willing implies thought and view of the heart. Right thinking is the effort put into directing all of your resources to one focused center. Right meditation is the mindfulness that can then become a part of your effect on the neighbors of the world around you. Right use of resources in life is the concentration of spiritual progress. Right treatment of others is the grounding of speech, action, and livelihood into an enlightened form of sharing in a'universal field of love.

The Dharma exists within many traditions with differing words and stories, names and histories, directions and expectations. The response of Jesus here to the question about what is the most valuable commandment of the Jewish Torah is exactly the reply that would be expected from a Buddhist frame of reference.

Determination

Hidden inheritance

The point in both versions is that we forever have a home, no matter how far away we have ventured, no matter how much we have forgotten. Home is home.

The Christ:

> There was a man that had a young son who asked for his inheritance, and the man gave him his share. Not long after this, the young son gathered his belongings and took off for a long journey. He went to a far away land where he spent his inheritance on worldly pleasures. As he spent the last of his inheritance, a depression came to that country. He found he had nothing. He went to work for a man who sent him into the fields to feed his pigs. He ate the husks that the pigs were eating. No one would help him.

> One day he woke up and realized that even the servants at his father's house had food to spare while he was starving in this far away land. He made up his mind to return to his father and tell him – Father, I have failed heaven and you. I am no longer worthy to be called your son. Make me one of your servants.

He got up and went back to his father. When he was still a long way off, his father saw him coming and felt compassion for him. The father ran out to greet him and hugged him and kissed him. The son said – Father, I have failed heaven and you. I am no longer worthy to be called your son...

The father called his servants. He instructed them to bring him the best clothes, put a ring on his finger, put shoes on his feet, and make a feast for his stomach. He proclaimed – This son of mine was dead, but he is alive again. He was lost, but he has been found.

The entire house began to celebrate. [Luke 15:12-24]

The Buddha:

A young man ran away from his father and lived for a long time in a far away land. Fifty years went by. The older he got, the poorer he became. He tried every direction, begging for food and warm clothing, wandering further and further from home. One day by chance he was journeying close to home. His father had searched for him for years. He was very wealthy. At last the son came to the town where his father lived. The father thought with regret and hope, since he was becoming old and weak, that there would be no one to inherit all of his wealth. He thought, if only he could find his lost son. The son came to his father's gate, but seeing the wealth and power of his father he departed. He went to a poor village to work. The father sent a servant to bring back his son. The son was afraid that he was being arrested. The father seeing his fear ordered that he be let go. He then sent his servants to offer the son a job that paid twice as much as he could make. He then visited his son in disguise, advising him to not be lazy in his work. Later he visited him and told him that he would provide him with everything he needed, adopting him as his very son. For twenty years the son thought of himself as an employed worker. When the father became ill and knew he was about to die, he told his son to take control of his wealth. The poor son managed the wealth, but didn't take any of it, not even the cost of a single meal. Near death, the father arranged a meeting with his relatives and told the story of the son who left home at a young age and came back as his servant. The son was overjoyed at having gained riches beyond anything he could have hoped for. [Lotus Sutra 4]

Sentient beings are like a man with a priceless gem hidden in his garment of which he is ignorant. He becomes poor and ragged and hungry and wanders about to distant lands. Although he is actually suffering from poverty, he still is in possession of the priceless gem. One day a very wise man tells the poor man of his priceless gem and from that time the poor man becomes very wealthy. [Surangama Sutra 1; also Lotus Sutra 8]

Resolve the impossible

All of the reasons why we can't step out and take the Dharma chance are not permanent obstacles. Where will is strong, things can change. The impossible begins to be seen as just the usual challenge. Forces begin to align and synchronize and make effective change in your world. Mindfulness is magic.

The Christ:

Your wishes fail you because you have zero faith. The truth I will tell you—with faith the size of a mustard seed you can command a mountain to move away and it will move. Nothing is impossible for you. [Matthew 17:20]

The Buddha:

A monk advanced in concentration can split the Himalayas in two. [Anguttara Nikaya 6:24]

Wanting

You get out of the Dharma what you put into it. In fact, you get out of anything what you put into it. Your state of resurrecting is dependant upon how much you want to elevate your consciousness. Your state of cleanliness is dependant upon how much energy you put into bathing. The Dharma is no different from any other pursuit. It requires that you put your energy into it in order for it to flourish in your life.

The Christ:

Ask for what you want to know. Search for what you want to find. Knock to open the shut doors. Everyone who asks a question will be given an answer. Everyone who searches will find what they have been longing for. To everyone who knocks the door shall be opened. [Matthew 7:7-8]

The Buddha:

Striving is the best thing you can do to finally arrive at the truth. If you do not strive, you will never arrive at the truth. Because you strive, you are guaranteed to eventually arrive at the truth. This is why striving is the best thing you can do to finally arrive at the truth. [Canki Sutta 22]

Open Dharma

DHARMA LESSON: Before John there was religion and prophecy, but then the Dharma has been preached and everyone is rushing toward it. [Luke 16:16]

A very brief and interesting line preserved in Luke, it was a literal crack at the Essene lifestyle. For over a century they had withdrawn into their private worlds of studying the Law and the Prophets, forming closed communities and not allowing outsiders to hear their teachings. John brought it all out into the open, publicly teaching the secrets of the Essenes, and possibly even those of the Alexandrine mystics. Now the outsiders have learned the truths and are forcing their way in. No more can there be an elitist *holier than thou* group behind the stone walls without the ruffians breaking in and demanding gnosis. It's as if John had broken into the secret vaults of the Vatican library and began to publish all of the mysteries of the Church. Now the walls are breaking down and the secrets are being preached from the rooftops.

The Law was a cold written statement of how it was in the past. The Prophets were cold written traditions of how it will be in the future. The Dharma is a warm living transforming present that can immediately alter both past and future, forgive sins, transform destinies, supercede Law and redirect Prophecy.

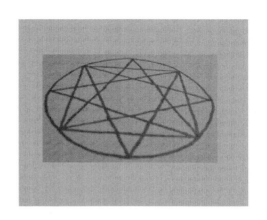

3. WHERE THE DHARMA GETS ITS FEET WET

Blessed is he who keeps his heart clean by not slandering with the tongue. Blessed is he who clings to his principles and shuns iniquity. [Dead Sea Scrolls 4Q525 Frag. 2 2:1-2]

The step beyond you are what you think about is you appear to stand for what you talk about. The Buddha presents right speech as the next Dharma foundation, immediately after right view and right selection. Dharma demands that we deal with life. We can't just stay up in the free will sky and soak up the sunrays all day. This is where we get our feet wet with having to come down to earth and interact with other people. The main way we begin to interact is communication. Our words represent the tone of our heart, our mood, our intent, our purpose, and our message. This is why communicating the Dharma comes before doing anything else with the Dharma.

Words are powerful tools. They can be used to encapsulate ignorance and perpetuate its existence. They can be used to express division, to rationalize injustice, to explain away prejudice, to justify a lack of compassion. Words may also be used to inspire the world with the Dharma of concern and hope and charity and transformation.

The Christ:

It is by words that you will be praised and by words that you will be condemned. [Matthew 12:37]

James — Anyone who does not trip up in speech has reached perfection and is able to keep the body on a tight rein. [James 3:2]

Do not make a big production of words. Simply say *yes* if you mean yes and *no* if you mean no. Anything beyond this just tempts trouble. [Matthew 5:34, Matthew 5:37]

The Buddha:

Do not engage in the many forms of pointless talking — of kings, criminals, politicians, armies, dangers, wars, food, drink, clothes, beds, flowers, perfumes, relatives, vehicles, villages, towns, cities, countries, women, heroes. They talk on the street and by the well. They talk about days gone by, rambling chitchat, and speculation, about everything on land and in the sea. They are always talking about this and that. [Saccasamyutta 10]

Words have weighed down all that there is. Nothing extends its rule further than that of words. Words are the one thing that has everything under its control. [Devatasamyutta 61]

When you attain quietness, the troubles of the world will go away. [Tao Te Ching 37]

Not so black and white

Limitations of legal words

It is not just about what you ever do and don't do. It is about truth, sincerity, honesty, authenticity, and compassion.

Showing the limitation of thinking only in terms of what is legal or not, black and white, the topic of divorce was used as an example of something that is perfectly legal but can have heartless effects on people. In that culture, a divorced woman's status was practically that of a prostitute. Even in today's world, divorce hurts everyone involved. Legally correct does not equal heartfully correct. It is like hogging up the left lane going the speed limit, thinking that anyone who wants to go faster would be breaking the law – legally correct, but extremely rude.

The Christ:

Do not imagine that I desire to break you away from the Law. I don't desire that you break away, but completely fulfill. The Law's purpose is achieved in a universal timeless achieving of what is written in tiny strokes of ink. [Matthew 5:18]

By a piece of paper with writing on it you can divorce your wife, sending her out alone in the world to become defiled and to defile any man she contacts. [Matthew 5:31-32]

The Buddha:

The Law says to not deceive or tell lies. If you refrain from killing, stealing, and adultery, keeping the thoughts of such out of mind, yet fails to be truthful and sincere, there will be no emancipation for you. [Surangama Sutra: Importance of Keeping the Precepts]

Defiling foods

No matter what you put into your mouth, it all comes out the same. Think about it before you flush. What comes out of your mouth is your speech, and you are in complete control of the honesty and purity of your conversations. You can't control what is spewing out on both ends, so concentrate on the end that you can take control over.

The Christ:

There is nothing that you can put into your mouth that defiles you. It is what comes out of your mouth that can be defiling. [Mark 7:15]

Eating without washing your hands is not what defiles you. [Matthew 15:20]

The Buddha:

Stealing, lying, and adultery—these defile, but not the eating of food. [Sutta Nipata 242]

Do not criticize religion

One of the greatest obstacles within religious paths is the tendency to define who you are in terms of not being like others who you see as ignorant and on the wrong path. This divides people in our minds. Concentrate on what is universal and illuminating. The Dharma does not come to take away the various traditions of people, but to respectfully add a light with which different type of people can discover their own version of the faith.

The Christ:

Do not imagine that I am here to speak against the Law or the Prophets. My purpose is not to speak against but to fulfill (pleroo – to complete, to make perfect, to accomplish). [Matthew 5:17]

The Buddha:

In explaining this sutra, take no delight in speaking of the limitations of any people with their scriptures. Display no contempt for the many ways that the Dharma is taught. [Lotus Sutra 14]

Hidden meanings

No complete truth

Beware of anyone's attempt to use words to completely encapsulate truth. If the Bible truly is God's message for the world, he has been silenced for the past couple of thousand years. What if He has something else to say and no one will now listen? Jesus met the same mentality in his day. Scripture came in a limited edition predefined package of just so many words and that was it.

Your verdict is God's quote from the Bible is an amazing jab at Fundamentalism that holds the Bible as being the complete word of

God. Jesus answered that if the words of people supplement the word of God, then new revelations can be presented, new insights offered. While the Brahmins had their *Vedas* well defined with no new entries to be made in the scriptures, and the Jews had their defined collection of writings that we now call the *Bible*, the message presented by both the Buddha and the Christ is that truth cannot be completely collected and carved into stone. If you limit what you define as truth, you stunt your spiritual growth. You have placed it as an obstacle in the way of your own spiritual progress.

The Christ:

Jews—We are stoning you for blasphemy, though you are only a man you claim to be God.

Christ—Is it not written in your Law "your verdict is God's"? [Deuteronomy 1:17] So the word God is applied to the people issuing the addresses of God. And you don't allow scripture to be set aside. [John 10:31-35]

The Buddha:

Brahmins—Only this is true. Anything else is false.

Buddha—The ancient Brahmin seers, the creators and composers of the ancient hymns that have been chanted (The ancient Hindu scriptures), spoken, and studied to this day, repeated for generations, did these ancient Brahmin seers think to themselves only this is true, anything else is false? [Canki Sutta 12-13]

Expedient teachings

Simply explain to the simple. No need for fancy philosophical arguments. Present easy stories with obvious points presented as examples of every day common sense. I think spiritual intellectuals dismissed both the Buddha and the Christ for presenting an answer that was so childishly simple that the depth of it was overlooked.

The use of parables for teaching is difficult to find in ancient Jewish writings, even in the Dead Sea Scrolls. That parables are a good method for teaching and that teaching itself is a miraculous event are Buddhist concepts going back centuries before the advent of Christianity, listed with the ability to demonstrate psychic powers and to telepathically know the thoughts of other people as evidences of enlightenment. [Kevaddha Sutta 3]

The Christ:

Using simple parables, he taught them the Word in so far as they were able to receive it. He taught nothing except for the parables. His disciples were given full explanations when they were alone together. [Mark 4:33-34]

The Buddha:

I will give you similes, for some who are wise can grasp the meaning conveyed by means of a simile. [Rathavinita Sutta 14, Payasi Sutta 9]

Words can be Dharma vitamins

Words can be mysteries for those who don't know how to listen to them and extract their meaning, like listening to foreigners conversing in a language not understood. In listening to conversations using technical terms, outsiders feel lost. If the subject is computers or medicine or engineering or any other specialty field, those who have not studied in the field are outsiders in the conversation. The uninitiated are lost, getting nothing out of the speech. Those with a little background, a slight clue, will pick up on the hidden meanings and rapidly advance.

Once the words explaining the Dharma are understood, you who have grasped the truth are forever changed, destined for a sanctified eternity. Words are powerful. Words are magical.

The Christ:

Light penetrates the darkness, and the darkness could not understand what was happening. [John 1:5]

I speak to them in parables. For you it is granted to comprehend the mysteries of the Dharma, but to them it is not granted. Those who have will be rewarded with excess. Those who have not will be rewarded with being deprived of the little they do have. I speak to them in parables. They stare without seeing. They hear the words but don't grasp the meaning. [Matthew 13:10-13]

Everyone who believes may attain eternal life. [John 3:15]

The Buddha:

The world's savior is beyond our ability to comprehend. Among the beings of heaven to the people of the earth to all living beings, none can contain the Buddha in his understanding. [Lotus Sutra 2]

When the hearers and bodhisattvas listen to the Dharma that I preach, as soon as they have grasped one sentence, they will without a doubt be assured of attaining Buddhahood. [Lotus Sutra 2]

Don't teach the unready

Spiritual truths are dangerous in the wrong minds. Narrow-minded people may consider your insights to be "of the devil" and may even turn against you in violence. Be careful who you reveal your deepest secrets to. The herd misunderstands mystical abilities and burns witches, excommunicates scientists, and crusades against mystics. Consider even today trying to explain in a church that you have discovered useful truths in paganism or in tarot or in kabbalah or in yoga. You will probably not be understood nor accepted and will quite probably be turned against. Watch your words for they are not for everyone out there. There is nothing you can do to get through to people who aren't open to listening to the Dharma.

The same words are heard by all. To those with the key, it is a great spiritual feeding. To those without the key, they see the teachings as parables, clever stories talking about some distant kingdom. Those insiders who have the gift, the key, understand what is being discussed has immediate relevance in the here-and-now daily life. The key opens up so much that would not otherwise be understood, that could have been and actually has been lost and forgotten throughout the centuries. The Dharma is a living way of being. In the ancient Mysteries, the initiates didn't just attend something to be observed, they departed with a new way of living, of participating in the Mysteries of life. They found their old ego trips and put them to bed, resurrecting into a newly awakened experience of life firsthand, on the cutting edge of will. It was a transforming experience that colored every encounter, every event faced from then on out. It was being born again into a new way of being. The use of the word Mysteries here would point the ancient reader to such thoughts. The Dharma was a transforming continuous form of teaching that guided the experiencer through life. The parables of Jesus, like the similes of Gotama, were on the surface just stories, but at the depth of an initiate they presented meanings that could instantly awaken the disciples to higher truths.

The Christ:

If you take what you consider to be the most holy and give it to a dog, he will just drag it off. He might even turn and bite you. If you give pearls to a pig, he will just walk on them and grind them in the mud. [Thomas 93, Matthew 7:6]

For you it is granted to comprehend the mysteries of the Dharma. [Matthew 13:11]

The secrets of the Dharma are only for the initiated. For outsiders, they only hear parables. [Luke 8:10]

This generation is like a marketplace of people ignoring the children. They played their music and you wouldn't dance. They sang sad songs and you wouldn't cry. John came fasting and sober and you called him possessed. The Son of Man came feasting and drinking and you called him a glutton and a drunk. It will eventually be known that the children are the wise ones. [Luke 7:31-35, Matthew 11:16-19]

The Buddha:

I expressly command you to not preach this sutra to those who are unwise. [Lotus Sutra 3]

Considered as a bright jewel given from a king, this sutra is to be highly honored. As such it is to be constantly guarded and protected and not recklessly revealed. [Lotus Sutra 14]

This sutra is the storehouse of the secret realization of the Buddhas. It must not be given to others without serious requirements of preparation. [Lotus Sutra 10]

They blame the silent and they blame the speaker. [Dhammapada 17:7]

Communicate

The Dharma is perhaps more about what you don't say. The secrets of the initiate must remain secret. But it is not like the ancient schools that would kill members who spoke their secrets. It is not like a degree of initiation into some secret order. The secrets of the Dharma are open to all to discover by the heart, by experiences, by observation, by intuition. The world out there is hung up on religious dogmas, scientific arguments, traditional conclusions, accepted standards, and statistical data. The ideas presented by small insignificant unauthorized people are not valued enough to be listened to. They only want parrots that can repeat back what they say. No wonder they never learn anything new.

Uncovered truth

No more of carefully guarded secrets. The Dharma gives a way to see through the blinders, discover the hidden meanings, find the way, and see the Light—as a personal experience that cannot be denied the experiencer.

The Christ:

> All now covered will be revealed. All now hidden will be made known. All hidden in darkness will be seen in the light. All quiet whispers will be shouted from the rooftops. [Matthew 10:26-27]

The Buddha:

> All fallen over will be set upright. All hidden will be revealed. All lost will find their way. All groping in the darkness will be given a lamp to hold up. [Culahatthipadopama Sutta 27]

The ready will accept

For all of the frustrations in trying to convey the Dharma to the world, there are those who are ready for it, who need to be introduced to it. They are eagerly waiting with attentive ears and clear eyes.

The Christ:

> If your vision is focused, your world will be filled with light. If your vision is scattered, your world will be filled with darkness. [Matthew 6:22-23]

The Buddha:

> There are those with little dust in their eyes who are missing out on being able to hear the Dharma. [Ariyapariyesana Sutta 20]

> Let the Blessed One teach the Dharma. There will be those who can understand. [Ariyapariyesana Sutta 20]

Proclaim

The Dharma is for sharing, for transforming the entire planet into a better place to live for us all. The missionary activity of the Buddhists brought the Dharma to where Jesus could take the torch and pass it on to those around him. The missionary activity of the Christians brought the gospels to us today, encapsulating the Dharma in the teachings of Jesus. Now it is up to this season's people to take the torch and pass it along as still relevant for the planet. The words may change once again with the change of the age and the culture, but the heart will forever remain that of the eternal and universal Dharma of the Way of Love.

This is the image we all have of the wandering monk as being a source of mystical teachings and divine powers of healing who had renounced possessions and conventional life. Possessing nothing of material worth, an elusive treasure was at his disposal. The simple wandering ascetic was a part of the very culture in the East, in Hindu, Buddhist, and Jainist areas. The expectation that charity is to be provided to begging monks was part of the Eastern cultures. It was becoming a part of the Essene Jewish culture, a network of communities that supported travelers within their own tradition (according to the accounts of the Essenes by Josephus). Strangers from other towns would be invited in to the home, fed, provided for, and listened to during the evening time of socializing. It was into this community oriented accepting culture that these Dharma teachers were sent. Into the private homes of those who would welcome them, they taught the intimate healing details of the Dharma. It was a one-on-one contact passing on of a living tradition to be shared through experience. There were more towns to visit than Dharma teachers to go around, so no time was to be wasted at unwelcome places.

The Christ:

I am sending you to proclaim the Dharma and to heal. Take nothing for the journey, neither staff, nor bag, nor bread, nor money, not even a spare tunic. Whatever house you enter, stay there. When you leave town, leave from that same house. If the first house you enter does not welcome you, shake their dust off of your feet as you leave their town. [Matthew 10:5-15, Mark 6:7-13, Luke 9:1-6]

The Buddha:

I send you forth, monks, to wander abroad for the good of the many, for the welfare and happiness of divas (angels) and humans. Display the holy live fully complete and perfect. There are beings with little dust on their eyes that are perishing through not hearing Dharma. They will become knowers of Dharma. [Mahapadana Sutta 3:26]

All disciples should be without possession with the exception of their poor clothing and begging bowls. [Surangama Sutra: Importance of Keeping the Precepts]

Walk, monks, across the lands so that the people may find blessing, so that the people may find joy, and so that the people may find compassion. Let not two of you follow the same path. [Mahavagga 1:11:1]

DHARMA LESSON: I was sent here with the purpose of proclaiming the good news (gospel) of the Dharma to the people in many towns. [Luke 4:42-43]

The crowds wanted to hold Jesus — define Jesus — limit Jesus. His reply to this was that his purpose, his mission, was this Dharma, this amazing Dharma, this important and valuable Dharma, this Dharma that was the purpose and mission of Jesus to teach, this Dharma that in itself is the gift of this Christ to the world. This Dharma is the religion of Jesus, for whatever this may have meant to Jesus. This Dharma was what Jesus gave to us as the means for us to resurrect ourselves into our eternal state of being. It should be the ultimate purpose of those who claim Jesus as their spiritual leader to discover what this Dharma means. This Dharma is the religion of Jesus.

DHARMA LESSON: Crowds followed Jesus. He welcomed them and talked about the Dharma, healing those who were sick. [Luke 9:11]

The Dharma was shared with the crowds by the Dharma Master. It was his purpose and message and ambition to share the Dharma with those who would accept it, breathe life into it, and transmit it through their own lives to those who could then accept it from them.

Word projection of heart

The orchard of trees is judged by its fruit the same as a person's feelings are judged by his words. [Sirach 27:6]

Anger yells out. Jealousy sobs. Envy snips. Insecurity criticizes. Frustration screams. A truly compassionate heart speaks comforting words. A truly caring soul speaks helpful words.

The Christ:

Grow a good tree and the fruit will be good. Grow a rotten tree and the fruit will be rotten. You judge a tree by the quality of its fruit. Can good words come out of evil people? Words flow from the heart. Good people flow out goodness from their store of goodness. Bad people flow out badness from their store of badness. [Luke 6:43-45, Matthew 12:33-36, Matthew 7:17-18, Thomas 45]

The Buddha:

Whatever a person does, be it good or evil, is never without consequence, for all deeds bear fruit of its own kind. [Udanavarga 9:8]

A corrupt seed will reveal itself in diseased and malformed fruit. [Surangama Sutra: Importance of Keeping the Precepts]

The truth is veiled

Truth is invisible to those who have defined how they look at the world. It is silent to those who have defined how they listen. Such great custodians of the Dharma that have lived in various cultures and ages were generally misunderstood and not very well received. What makes people with good ears not be able to hear is that they refuse to listen. Those who are convinced that they hold in their hand all that they need to know will not be open to listening.

The Christ:

He came to his own people and they did not accept him. [John 1:11]

The Buddha:

The appearance of a Buddha in the world is rare and difficult to take place. When they do appear, it is often difficult for them to preach the Dharma. [Lotus Sutra 2]

Inspiration

The Dharma is channeled as a force greater than any one of us. The aligning force of those who have turned the Dharma Wheel in the past will keep it in its proper motion. Catholic Christianity calls this the communion of saints. In the Far East there is the idea of being guided by the ancestors. For however we think about it, the message presented is that we are not alone. The same Spirit of the Father that worked for those disciples of Jesus centuries ago is still driving the same Dharma today. The languages are different and we have advancements in communication and technology, but the Dharma message remains the same. It is alive in each of our hearts and all we have to do is to tap into it and let it flow through our expression of it.

Inspiration protection

The Christ:

It is not you who are speaking, but the Spirit of your Father that is blowing through you. [Matthew 10:20]

The Buddha:

When they preach this Dharma they will make no mistake...for this sutra is protected by the supernatural powers of all of the Buddhas of the past, present, and future. [Lotus Sutra 14]

Eternal Dharma

Some may like to think of this planet as solid and lasting, but it will eventually cease to exist. It may last for millions or billions of more years, but it revolves around a dying star. The point is that eternity is relative for everything that is put together and conditional. Only the Dharma is truly forever.

The Christ:

Sky and earth will eventually cease to be, but my words will live forever. [Mark 13:31]

The Buddha:

The vast world will burn up, being completely destroyed and ceasing to exist. [Anguttara Nikaya 7:62]

Express suffering

To be honestly heartfelt miserable is better than being artificially happy. The content never seek for comfort. If the voice is to be used for anything within the Dharma Path, it is to be used to cry out for truth, for enough compassion to be created to balance out the suffering and pain in the world.

The Christ:

Bless you who mourn for you will find comfort. [Matthew 5:5]

The Buddha:

I wish for you that you remain untroubled and that no reason for delight ever be found in you. Delight comes to you who are miserable. Misery comes to you who are delighted. [Devaputtasamyutta 18]

4. WHERE THE DHARMA HITS THE DIRT

> Do not unto others what you would not wish done to you. [Tobit 4:15]

> What is hateful to yourself do not to your fellow man. That is the whole of the Torah and the remainder is but commentary [Hillel: Shab 31a (Talmud)]

Become God in your own world. Where else could you be God? Encounter God in your own world. Where else could you meet God? Become the eyes of God to observe what needs to be helped in the world. Become the hands of God to actually make a difference. The Buddha was too busy putting compassion into practice to worry about theological arguments about God. Jesus was too busy with *hands on* compassion defining his Father to worry about theological debates of the rabbis. In other words, God within the Dharma is a verb and not a noun. God is met by doing God.

> The soul seems to be God and God seems to be the soul. [St. John of the Cross: Spiritual Canticle 31:1]

> The soul appears to be God more than a soul. Indeed it is God by participation. [St. John of the Cross: The Ascent of Mount Carmel II 4:7]

The fourth spoke of the Dharma Wheel is life in the world out there. It is present after the foundation of having taken the spark of the Dharma, formed an inner resolving of intent to represent the Dharma, and learning how to communicate the Dharma. If it is all just mind games, it can be dismissed as so much fluff. If there is any validity at all to the Dharma, it must have an impact out there on the streets of life. It must mean something in real life.

Expect to see the Dharma

Science has taught us to believe only in that which we can observe the impact of its presence. If there is any truth at all to the Dharma then it can be measured and touched, calculated and applied. If nothing physical ever changed due to the metaphysical, the Dharma could be dismissed as yet another blind faith in bogus promises of deluded people. If the physical world synchronizes and lines up and gives feedback in the forms of intuitive signs, then it is known that there is more to reality than the forms of energy that have mass.

Physical alignment

You are not going through it alone. With the Dharma as your companion and purpose and destination, obstacles and hindrances fall aside to allow you to continue your quest. Watch the synchronicity.

Watch the coincidences. Watch the world align a path for you. The storms will blow past and you will still be there on the other side. Supernatural forces guide impossible tasks. The world changes from being a set of walls into being a set of bridges to help you along the Way.

The Christ:

Peter: Lord if it is you, tell me to walk on the water to you.

Jesus: Come.

Then Peter got out of the boat and walked toward Jesus across the water. [Matthew 14:28-29]

He got into the boat with the disciples and the wind stopped. [Mark 6:51]

The Buddha:

Anyone who fulfils the precepts may wish to walk on water without sinking as though it was earth and such a supernatural power may be held. [Akankheyya Sutta 14]

Having crossed over himself, he leads others across. [Upali Sutta 29]

If clouds should thunder and lightening and hail and rain, think of the power of that Hearer of Sounds and at that moment the storm will end. [Lotus Sutra 25]

Reality check

Dharma is about doing. Viewing and intending and talking get you so far. If you don't act like a child of the Dharma, then you are not.

The Christ:

Any tree that does not produce good fruit is cut down and used as firewood. All are judged by their fruits. [Matthew 7:19-20]

Why do you call after me "Lord, Lord" and refuse to follow my instructions? [Luke 6:46]

The Buddha:

Beings are owners of their actions. They are heirs of their actions. They are as they have become because of their actions. They are not separable from their actions. Their home is their actions. It is actions that distinguish beings as small or great. [Culakammavibhanga Sutta 4]

Invisible revelation

It is how you go about looking for miracles that determines whether or not you will see miracles. If miracles were that obvious then there would be no one who could doubt. The key is to be amazed with what cannot be seen or shown. People from various religious traditions around the world experience miracles every day. What they usually have in common is that those who don't experience the miracles can nearly always explain away the events. Those who witnessed the miracles have no way to prove it or to demonstrate it to the skeptics.

The Christ:

Jesus said with a deep sigh—Why do this people demand a sign? In truth I tell you that no sign shall be given to this people. [Mark 8:12]

The Buddha:

There are two conditions for the attainment of the signless deliverance of mind—the ignoring of all signs and the paying attention to the element beyond signs. [Mahavedalla Sutta 27]

Value of friends

Friendship is the greatest treasure discovered out there in the world. People can help each other along in times of need.

The Christ:

The dishonest accountant who was about to be fired conceived of a plan to take care of his future. He lowered the debt of many who owed and instantly became their friends. The master could only give him praise for his cunning. This world gives more opportunity for making deals than does the realm of light. [Luke 16:1-8]

The Buddha:

By giving, friendship is bound. By this you never sorrow with passing away from this life to the next. [Yakkhasamyutta 12]

Fight Dharma obstacles

Anyone who completely follows the Law without deviating will be accepted by God as an offering of an atoning sacrifice and be accepted into the New Testament of the Eternal Unity (Yahad). [Dead Sea Scrolls 1QS 3:10-12]

Guided by the instruction of the Holy Spirit, they shall become an atonement for the guilt of transgression. For the rebellion of sin, they shall become an acceptable sacrifice for the land, just as the burnt offerings. Prayer shall become the very means for grace to be attained, the sweet odor of righteous and holy lives will be considered to be a pleasing freewill offering. [Dead Sea Scrolls 1QS 9:4-5]

It is notable when an event finds its place in all four gospels. The story was well known in circles of people that didn't communicate with one another. It was the universal image of Jesus, the Rabbi gone mad. Hosea 6:6 already had the concept of what God really wants is a people that show compassion, not people that sacrifice animals. [Matthew 9:13] From the Dead Sea Scrolls of his day we read that living a righteous life was thought to itself be a free will offering, a spiritual sacrifice. If we see Jesus as having the radical vision of transforming Judaism from a religion based on ritual animal sacrifice in the Temple to a religion based on community compassion, then this seemingly violent act becomes understood as being that of a man impassioned with a transforming vision of change. The explanations that he was only concerned with the money involved don't seem to fully explain the situation. His answer that follows in the gospel texts is that this Temple won't last but the Temple of his body will live forever. What may should be obvious, but is not due to Christian theology getting in the way, is that the *body of Christ* that is the eternal Temple is none other than the disciples who live for the Dharma. They are the community that presents itself as a living sacrifice. This is the vision of Jesus for his Church, for his body. The body is the Church, the Sangha. In Buddhism there are *three jewels* – the Buddha, the Dharma, and the Sangha. It could be thought of in Christian terms – the Christ, the Dharma, and the Church. The purpose of the Church is to continue the Dharma of the Christ.

The Christ:

Jesus went to the Jerusalem Temple up to the vendors selling cattle and sheep and doves, with their piles of money. Making a whip out of rope, he chased them all out of the Temple, freed the sheep and cattle, threw their money, knocked over their tables and the dove sellers seats, saying — Take all of this out of here and stop using my Father's house as a business. He stopped anyone trying to carry sacrifices through the Temple. [John 2:13-16, Matthew 21:12-13, Mark 11:15-17, Luke 19:45-46]

The Buddha:

At a sacrifice at which no oxen are slain, nor goats, birds, pigs, nor any other animal, but where the people there have the right view, the right thought, the right speech, the right action, the right livelihood, the right effort, the right mindfulness, and the right concentration, then the sacrifice is of plentiful fruit and profit, shining with a majestic Light. [Payasi Sutta 31]

Non-violence

I vow to never repay evil with evil. I will only seek out a man for good. [Dead Sea Scrolls 1QS 10:17-18]

Dharma does not come by forcing itself. Dharma can never contact the world with violence. Dharma should never cause pain. Any religious force that invaded and conquered and forced conversions does not represent the true Dharma. Jesus never led a crusade.

A tradition about hands and gestures was used as a teaching tool by Jesus that eludes modern audiences. Someone striking you on your right cheek is using the left hand as a sign of contempt, of provocation to fight back. The left hand was reserved for all unclean uses, such as going to the bathroom. In turning to the left cheek, you are then welcoming the right hand that would caress in friendship, as a sign of comradeship. The right hand was reserved for eating and greeting. What Jesus was saying was to offer friendship to those who are mistreating you. Look beyond the violence and bigotry that currently has them trapped.

The Christ:

Put away your sword. All who use a sword will die by a sword. [Matthew 26:52]

The thought of *an eye for an eye and a tooth for a tooth* needs to be abandoned. [Matthew 5:38, Exodus 21:24]

Offer no resistance to the wicked. If someone strikes you on your right cheek, turn and offer the other cheek as well. [Matthew 5:39]

React to a man who is taking your coat by giving him the shirt off of your back. [Matthew 5:40]

React to someone rudely imposing you to go a mile by going an extra mile. [Matthew 5:41]

Never refuse to help anyone who asks you to help them. Never turn away anyone who comes to you in need. [Matthew 5:42]

Love your enemies. Pray for those who threaten you with violence. [Matthew 6:44]

How often should you forgive someone who does you wrong? Seven times? Could you forgive the same person seventy times seven times? [Luke 17:3-4]

The Buddha:

Those who take swords and shields and buckle on bows and quivers, charging into battle with arrows and spears flying and swords flashing — they will be found run through with arrows and spears, their heads cut off by swords. [Mahadukkhakklandha Sutta 12]

A killer's child becomes a killer. A conqueror's child becomes a conqueror. An abuser's child becomes an abuser. A reviler's child becomes a reviler. The way that karma unfolds, the plunderer will eventually be plundered. [Kosalasamyutta 15]

You should train yourself to remain unaffected of mind, without uttering any evil words, abiding with compassion for the welfare of others, with a mind of loving kindness, with no trace of inner hate.

If anyone should give you a blow with his hand, with a rock, with a stick, or with a knife, you should abandon any revengeful thoughts or words. [Kakacupama Sutta 6]

Even if bandits cut you limb from limb with a saw, the arising in the mind of hatred towards them would not be doing as I have taught you. [Kakacupama Sutta 20]

When men beat you and scold you, you must accept it patiently. With hands pressed together bow to them humbly. [Surangama Sutra: Importance of Keeping the Precepts]

To anger, respond with peacefulness. To evil, respond with good. To greed, respond with giving. To lies, respond with truth. [Dhammapada 17:3]

Be tolerant with the intolerant. Be patient with the harsh. The holy man shows compassion to all creatures. [Udanavarga 33:46]

Respond to hatred with kindness. [Tao Te Ching 63]

You who strike back at one striking you, who scream back at one screaming at you, who plot against the one who plots against you, have already swallowed the bait, already lost control. We do not swallow the bait. We do not lose control. [Brahmanasamyutta 2]

You who repay an angry man with anger only make things worse for yourself. By not repaying an angry man with anger, you become the victor of a difficult battle. [Sakkasamyutta 4]

Dharma protects those who act intelligently

Keep the fangs of the world at a safe distance. As long as you remain in control of the situation, nothing can harm you. Dharma expects you to be intelligent enough not to do something stupid.

The Christ:

Here is a sign that you are entrusted — you will know how to pick up a snake. Deadly poison is no threat to anyone who can heal with the touch of his hands. [Mark 16:18]

The Buddha:

A wise man saw a large snake. Catching it with a stick, he grasped it by the neck. The snake may wrap its coils around his hand or arms or legs, but he could not die or suffer from that. He is safe because he is correctly grasping the snake. [Alagaddupama Sutta 11]

Swords and staves will not touch and poison will have no power to harm. [Lotus Sutra 14]

If lizards, snakes, vipers, scorpions threaten you with poison breath that burns like fire, think of the power of that Hearer of Sounds and your voice will cause them to flee. [Lotus Sutra 25]

Stay pure

Protect those you love from the effects of contact with the world. What we need to wash away from each other's lives is the pain, the guilt, the intolerances that discriminate against, the unfair laws and political structures in place — wash away whatever distracts from the Dharma. Wash them until they are clean and beautiful.

The Christ:

A woman washed the feet of Jesus with her tears, wiping them with her hair, anointing them with ointment. [Luke 7:38, John 12:3]

Jesus poured water into a basin and washed his disciples' feet. [John 13:5]

Understand what I have done for you. I am rightfully called your master and lord, and yet I have washed your feet. So too must you wash each other's feet. [John 13:13-14]

The Buddha:

Buddha sat down on the seat prepared for him and washed his feet. [Culagosinga Sutta 5]

You don't become pure by washing in the same fashion as the many mortals of the world. You become pure by washing away sins. [Udanavarga 33:13]

Love conquers hate

Compassion is the antibiotic for ill will. If you can expand the group who you *feel for* to even include your enemies, your persecutors, to bad and good alike, to those who show you no compassion — then you can attain a perfect state of limitless love. Such a love is liberating, resurrecting, freeing, evolving, and healing. Kindness opens up yourself to include others in your life. Out in the world you are given the opportunities to grow your Dharma Nature.

Tradition had it that charity was to be given only for the devout humble good folk, for *one of us* and not for *one of them*. The godless sinner was not to be the object of charity. They are not to be given a piece of bread. They only deserve the wrath of God. [Sirach 12:1-7] The "yeah, but..." that was inserted into this context was most probably that of a conscientious young objector called Jesus. The God of Jesus was the One who caused the sun to shine upon and the rain to fall upon the bad and the good alike. [Matthew 5:45] Then Jesus presented the summary of his message in this one simple Law.

Dharma is *unconditional* compassion, unstoppable joy, untiring strength, and untroubled peace. Dharma only responds with love, with acts of kindness, with blessings and prayers for the betterment of others. The inner source of Dharma has to be understood as being greater than any situation forced out there in the world.

The Dharma supplies people for the world that know how to pay attention and care, that envision changes for a better world and then work for those changes, that see the needs of people and supply them with what they are needing. Such open hearted giving service to the world in turn inspires faith in the Dharma. Here is the way to fly in the Dharma love, not love that only desires to experience or that wishes well, but a love that actively makes a positive substantial impact in other people's lives.

Compassion takes away selfish pride, giving us hope for creating a world ruled by love. To let go of greed allows for charity, which is automatic if you love your neighbor as yourself. To lose arrogant selfishness inspires faith in the world being as one self-sustained united community guided by love. Dreams have to start somewhere.

The Christ:

Deal with others in the way that you would prefer for them to deal with you. [Matthew 7:12, Luke 6:31]

You should love your neighbor as you love yourself. [Matthew 19:19, Matthew 22:39, Leviticus 19:18]

Love even your enemies. Pray for even your persecutors. This is the way to being children of your heavenly Father. The sun shines on the bad as well as on the good. The rain falls on the righteous as well as on the wicked. If you love only those who love you, how are you any better than the worst of men? If you are friendly only to those of your own family, how are you setting an exceptional example for the world? Be completely perfect (teleios) as your heavenly Father is completely perfect. [Matthew 5:44-48]

This is my one commandment: love one another as I have shown love to you. [John 15:12, John 13:34]

It is by your love for one another that you will be globally recognized as being one of my disciples. [John 13:35]

Love one another since love is from God. Everyone who loves is a child of God and experiences God. Whoever fails to love cannot experience God because God is love. [1 John 4:7-8]

Anyone who loves his brother has discovered the Light and nothing can take this away from him. [1 John 2:10]

The Buddha:

There is the liberation of mind through love. Frequently giving careful attention to it is the poison that prevents new ill will from growing and existing ill will from thriving. [Bojjhangasamyutta 51]

Each person treats himself very dearly. Just as you would not harm yourself, you should not harm others. [Kosalasamyutta 8]

Consider no distinction between yourself and the selfhood of others. Practice charity by giving not just tangible gifts, but also the selfless gifts of kindness and charity. [Diamond Sutra 23]

Responding with more hate never defeats hate. Even in this world, hate can be conquered only by compassion. This is the Eternal Dharma. [Dhammapada 1:5]

We should live with joy and love among those who hate. We should live with joy and health among those who are ill. We should live in joy and peace among those who dwell on conflict. [Dhammapada 15:1-3]

He abused me, he struck me, he defeated me, he robbed me—in those who give a home to such feelings hatred will never be conquered. In this world hatred is never conquered by further acts of hate. It is conquered by hating hate itself. This is an ancient dharma carved in stone. [Upakkilesa Sutta 6]

Above, below, across—everywhere, to all as to yourself, dwell pervading the entire planet with a mind balanced in love, abundant, exalted, and limitless, with no traces of any hostility or ill will. [Cittasamyutta 7, Vatthupama Sutta 16]

With minds remaining unaffected, we should never speak harshly. We should be actively compassionate for the welfare of others. We should possess a mindset of loving-kindness, with no trace of hidden spite. We shall live facing one another with a mind immersed in loving-kindness, and starting with the person next to us, we shall live facing the entire planet with a mind immersed in loving-kindness. In abundance, exalted, without limit, without hostility, without ill will, we should thus train ourselves. [Kakacupama Sutta 11]

The Way has three treasures, a compassion that inspires hope, an economy that inspires charity, and a humility that inspires faith. To fail in compassion makes you bold. To fail in economy makes you greedy. To fail in humility makes you arrogant. [Tao Te Ching 67]

To attain a heart perpetually filled with loving kindness, filled to overflowing, with no room left neither for hatred nor for ill will, this liberating heart of loving-kindness is the way to union with Brahma (God). [Tevijja Sutta 76-77]

Serve

Caring for the sick and suffering of the world is a definite sign of being full of the Dharma. Mother Teresa should be remembered for representing Christ's Dharma in the world. To work for the benefit of others is the flowing of the Dharma. Flowers only grow from being rooted down in the dirt. To work for praise or prestige or control or appearances is the wilting of the Dharma, just as a heat lamp on a flower will cause it to wilt and die.

The Christ:

The greatest of you are you who are serving. Those who think highly of themselves can be quickly ignored. It is those who remain humble that you should take notice of. [Matthew 23:11-12]

The Buddha:

Be like water, choosing the lowest place, being of the greatest use, being kind and courteous, resonating with the good in others, speaking only true and kind words, seeking peace and order, striving to do your best, and being willing to yield to change. [Tao Te Ching 8]

The Perfect Sage rises above his people because of his humility. He comes to be their leader because he presents himself as their servant. [Tao Te Ching 66]

Charity is Dharma food

The more you give of yourself, the more Dharma grows in you. *Giving* is the foundation for building a great Dharma tower of a well-lived life.

A practical social gospel is greater than philosophical dogma debates. Dharma is dogma that is taken out for a walk and lived. Real Dharma makes a real impact on the world around it.

The Christ:

Go back and tell John that the blind see, the lame walk, the lepers are cleansed, the deaf hear, the sick and dying live in health, the good news is given to the Poor. Blessed is anyone who doesn't miss encountering me. [Luke 7:22-23, Matthew 11:4-5]

Pharisees—Why does the master eat with tax collectors and sinners?

Jesus—It is not the healthy that need the doctor, but the sick. Learn why mercy is more holy than sacrifice. I am not here to instruct the holy but to call out to the sinners. [Matthew 9:10-13]

How you treat the least of my brothers is how you treat me. [Matthew 25:40]

Give to anyone who asks you. If people want to borrow from you, don't turn them away. [Matthew 5:42]

Be generous and there will be rewards for you—filled up, packed in, shaken down, filled to overflowing, pouring out into your lap. How you measure out your giving is how your reward will be measured out. [Luke 6:38, Matthew 7:2]

The Buddha:

The sick are healed, the hungry and thirsty no longer know hunger and thirst, the addicts lose their addiction, the insane recover their sanity, the blind regain their sight, the deaf regain their hearing, the crippled and lame recover perfect limbs, the poor become rich, and the prisoners are set free. [Lalitavistra Sutra 7]

62

Those who want to stand by me should stand by those who are the most in need. [Mahavagga 8,26,3]

Possess a mind devoid of the stain of stinginess, being freely generous, open-handed, delighting in relinquishment, devoted to charity, delighting in giving and sharing. [Sotapattisamyutta 6]

You who give food, drink, clothing, transportation, pleasant surroundings, beds, homes, or lights to the homeless, wherever reborn will be wealthy. [Culakammavibhanga Sutta 14]

Healing

Therapeuo is the Greek word usually translated as heal. It also carries the connotation of waiting on, relieving, caring for, providing therapy for, and promoting a healing of the sick. *Nosos* is the Greek word usually translated as sick, meaning diseased or having a disability. *Malakia* is the Greek word usually translated as disease, implying a softness, a weakness, requiring soft clothing and requiring special care. The *Therapeutae* was a group of religious people in Alexandria, Egypt that lived in the century before Jesus. They were so called because they used herbs and techniques for healing the sick as part of their spirituality. It has been suggested by some scholars that Buddhist missionaries influenced them and that they in turn influenced the Essenes and thus the early Christians. That the Dharma of Jesus was presented as a healing ministry is an important realization. Ignorance (the ability to ignore) is the ultimate sickness while compassionate awareness is the ultimate cure. Ignorance is a disability of being that makes it difficult to make any spiritual progress, a weakness of constitution. Often the effect of having a weakness of constitution is shown in having a sick and weak body. The demons, created by the ignorance of being led around by desires for transient things, have to be exorcised. As any doctor can tell you, curing the symptom is not curing the disease. The source of the problem has to be eradicated. If someone has high blood pressure, the pills are not a cure. The source of the stress has to be identified. If someone is an alcoholic, aspirin is not a cure. Healing goes deep to a spiritual level of realigning the will, of enabling the disabled, or firming up the softness, of establishing a foundation (a Dharma) for growth and health.

Dharma is healing. Try not to think so much of a charismatic magical prevention of sickness and death. Instead think of a compassion that cleans and feeds and treats and encourages and aligns and works for the health and well being of all that it encounters. Hope can be magic in its own way, positive thinking being an amazing healing force.

This is the very act of preaching the Dharma. The message was not given in words, but in deeds of measurable compassion and charitable therapy.

The Christ:

He went around the villages teaching. He summoned twelve and sent them out two by two, giving them instructions over unclean spirits to drive them out and to heal all types of disease and illness. He sent them out to proclaim the Dharma and to heal the sick. [Matthew 10:1, Mark 6:7-8, Luke 9:1-2]

Proclaiming the good news of the Dharma, tend to the disabled and the weak. [Matthew 9:35]

The Buddha:

In time of sickness, the pure bodhisattvas prescribe the perfect holy medicine, causing all to become healthy and joyful, freed from their sickness. In time of hunger, they offer food and drink, stopping hunger and thirst, thus teaching the Dharma to healthy beings. [Vimalakirtinirdesha Sutra 8]

Avoid hypocrisy

Don't identify with your virtues any more than you identify with your bad qualities. Become detached, floating through your own life, an instrument for the Dharma to use, but not as an image for Dharma to be limited by. Once you try to look the part, you have lost the essence of Dharma.

The Christ:

When you are virtuous, your left hand must not know your right hand's charity. Your virtue must be in secret. Your Father who sees all that is done in secret will then reward you. [Matthew 6:3-4]

The Buddha:

You who are truly virtuous do not identify with your virtue. [Samanamandika Sutta 11]

Build sanctified presence

Physical success of Dharma rests upon the foundations laid, the *house* built around the spirit—the effects of the holy life being lived. The holy life protects from the floods to come. Right action is the solid foundation with the strong roof making your *house* withstand the storms to come.

Build a foundation for your own salvation

When a man wants to build a room, he coats it with plaster and covers it with a roof so it will not fall apart during the first hard rain. [Dead Sea Scrolls 4Q424 1:3-4]

The Christ:

Why bother following me around, crying, "Lord, Lord" when you don't follow my instructions? Everyone who comes to me and listens to my instructions and acts on them is like a man building a house that dug deep and laid a foundation on solid rock. The river rose and flooded the house, but it stood still. It was not shaken. Everyone who listens to my instructions and does nothing about it is like a man building a house on top of sand with no foundation. As soon as the river sends its flood it will collapse in utter ruin. [Luke 6:47-49]

The Buddha:

As rain pours into a house with a bad roof, so passion pours into an uncultivated spirit. As no rain can enter a house with a good roof, so passion can find no way into a cultivated spirit. [Dhammapada 1:13-14]

Charity to Dharma

As the Law has spoken, give charity to *The Poor*. Do not let *The Poor* leave without their needs in hand. Better to spend your money on a good brother than to leave it under a rock to rust away. Use your money as the Most High has commanded and you will find a treasure worth more than gold. Stock up your storerooms with charity, and you will be protected from misfortune. [Sirach 29:9-12]

You have to especially look out for those who have dedicated their lives to the Dharma. Support the holy orders of Dharma missionaries in whatever form you may encounter them.

The Christ:

The offering of a cup of water to one belonging to Christ will most assuredly be rewarded. [Mark 9:41, Matthew 10:42]

The Buddha:

The offerings of those who give to one who fulfils the precepts give the giver great fruit and benefit—whether the gift is clothing, food, a place to sleep, or medicine. [Akankheyya Sutta 5]

If there is anyone who offers alms to them and praises them, then in this present life there will be much blessing because of it. [Lotus Sutra 28]

Universal Dharma torch

Once again we have the same original Jewish Torah repeated, the same stone tablets taken down from the mountain by Moses. Actually these truths predate Moses, being universal and timeless and obvious. Compassion does not strike out or kill. Compassion does not take a man's wife behind his back. Compassion does not steal from a friend. Compassion does not speak words that harm others. Compassion is not greedy. Compassion looks out for family, for neighbors, for the community, and ultimately for the entire planet.

Judaism has been such a pivotal point in the Dharma because of its ancient collection of ethical rules called the Torah. The very lasting vision of Judaism is that cultures can be built up around the agreement on the Law of how people should interact. While Christianity emphasizes the notion of St. Paul that we should somehow get beyond the ancient Law, we find Jesus echoing its precepts back as a requirement for continuing along the Way that he was presenting. Even Buddha here sounds like a wise old Jewish rabbi. These truths were collected by various cultures including Judaism after literally thousands of years of observing that if we are nice to each other that it is better all around for all of us. Where the Dharma hits the dirt, the Law remains the same as when Moses began collecting these precepts long before the Buddha or the Christ began teaching.

The Christ:

You know the Law. Do not kill. Do not commit adultery. Do not steal. Do not bear false witness. Do not defraud. Do not dishonor your parents. [Mark 10:19-20]

If you want to find your life, keep the commandments. Do not kill. Do not commit adultery. Do not steal. Do not speak falsehoods against anyone. Honor your parents. Love your neighbors. [Matthew 19:17-19]

The Buddha:

Do not be cruel. Do not kill living beings. Do not take what is not given to you. Do not concern yourself with sexual conquests. Do not speak false words. Do not speak maliciously. Do not speak harshly. Do not gossip. Do not covet. Do not hold to ill will. Do not hold to wrong views. Do not hold to wrong intentions. Do not hold to wrong speech. Do not hold to wrong action. Do not keep a bad job. Do not continue in wrong effort. Do not continue in wrong mindfulness. Do not continue in wrong concentration. Do not continue in wrong knowledge. Do not continue in wrong deliverance. Do not be overcome by laziness and inactivity. Do not be restless. Do not be doubtful. Do not be angry. Do not be revengeful. Do not be contemptuous. Do not be domineering. Do not be envious. Do not be greedy. Do not be fraudulent. Do not be deceitful. Do not be stubborn. Do not be arrogant. Do not be difficult to admonish. Do not keep bad friends. Do not be negligent. Do not be faithless. Do not be shameless. Do not abandon fear of wrongdoing. Do not be shallow in thinking. Do not be lazy. Do not be unmindful. Do not be lacking in wisdom. Do not be stubborn in clinging to views. [Sallekha Sutta 12]

The Noble Discipline that leads to the cutting off of affairs — refrain from the killing of living beings, refrain from taking what has not been rightfully given to you, refrain from speaking falsely, refrain from speaking maliciously, refrain from rapacious greed, refrain from spiteful scolding, refrain from angry despair, and refrain from arrogance. [Potaliya Sutta 4]

Refrain from killing, from taking what is not given to you, from being unchaste, from speaking falsehoods, and from being swayed by gold and silver. [Khuddakapatha 2]

67

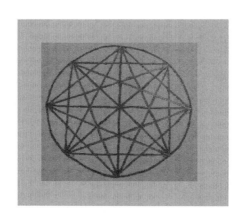

5. WHERE THE DHARMA LEARNS TO SWIM WITHOUT GETTING CAUGHT

> Hear the Dharma sown in the heart. Some don't understand and lose it. Some are too shallow and give it up. Some are so lost in the weeds of their desires that the Dharma gets choked. [Matthew 13:19]

Some are caught up in delusions, paradigms from which the Dharma makes no sense. It is some alien evil to them, a joke, like meat eaters making fun of vegetarians or couch potatoes making fun of exercisers. Some are just not evolved enough to consider the ethics presented in the light of riding the waves of their anger and frustrations with managing the immediate needs of their life. Some are carried along by the wishes for pleasant experiences, working for the money to pay for their toys, always wanting more and more. No time for the Dharma. These are the same as the three snares as taught by the Buddhists — *ignorance, hatred, and greed.*

The Buddha taught that the next step after learning how to talk the Dharma and walk the Dharma is to make sure you remain authentic and know what you stand for in life. This means that you are not allowed to sell out for money or fame or power. In the world and yet not of the world, the student of Dharma is like a fish swimming down a stream full of fishhooks. The shiniest hooks with the most appealing baits often turn out to come from organized religions themselves. Sometimes *being real* comes with a sacrifice that needs to be made.

Don't sell out

Control of wealth is the first shiny hook, the first temptation that both the Christ and the Buddha had to get past.

Don't sell out

In the Buddhist scriptures, Mara is the devil trying to tempt Gotama away from his mission of being the Buddha. The same three temptations are presented as the devil presents to Jesus in trying to tempt him away from his mission.

The Christ:

Devil — Follow me to the highest mountain and I will show you the riches of the world. I grant that you have the power to partake of their splendor. It is mine and belongs to the one that I choose. Honor me and it shall all belong to you.

Christ — You must honor the Lord God and treasure him alone. [Luke 4:5-8]

The Buddha:

Mara — May the Enlightened One now reign as king, the Perfected One rule with justice. If the Enlightened One spoke to the largest mountain in the Himalayas, the mountain would turn into gold. [Mahaparinibbana Sutta]

Mara — If the Blessed One wishes, he need only resolve that the largest of the Himalayan Mountains turn into gold and it would happen.

Buddha — How could a person turn to sensual pleasures that has known the source for suffering? Knowing acquisition as bondage in this world, I should rather wish for it to disappear. [Marasamyutta 20]

Get real

DHARMA LESSON: A man had two sons. He asked the first son to help him in his vineyard, but he refused. Later on he felt guilty and went to help. The man asked his second son to help him in his vineyard, and he agreed. Later on he was distracted and never went to help. Which of the two did what the Father wanted? [Matthew 21:28-31]

Is it better to talk about getting it or to actually get it? There are people that don't talk about themselves as even being religious who are embracing the Dharma in their very lives. There are people that continuously talk about being religious who are missing out on the Dharma. Better that people *get* the Dharma and thus change their ways than that people get trapped in spiritual mind games thinking they're righteous.

Hypocrites on ego trips

Watch out for anyone who thrives on the respect of people. Like crooked politicians or greedy television evangelists, if it is all about image and nothing about substance, it is shallow and distracting from the Dharma.

70

The Christ:

They thrive on sitting in places of honor at banquets and on the front row in the synagogues, greeted with respect in the market place and being called Rabbi by the people. [Matthew 23:6-7]

The Buddha:

They want the respect of others, wanting to be seen as superior, greedily watching over the offerings of the people. [Surangama Sutra: Importance of Keeping the Precepts]

Radical change of values

The cutting down and burning of fruitless trees is *so* not about sending people to hell. The Buddhist parallel here is very illuminating for the long misunderstood quote of John the Baptist. If we think of our lives as being orchards and the clearing away of the bad trees as being self-improvement, then we begin to understand the importance of the set of values that we cling to. Reduce, simplify, cut back, and uncomplicate your life. You get spread way too thin until your life gets far too cluttered with twisted fruitless trees (concerns) cluttering up the orchard of your life. It is time to do some gardening.

Better to enter the Dharma at all cost. Enter is eiserchomai in Greek, meaning the motion that places one into the accompanying of the destination. To cut off distractions that could lead you to a hell state instead is very central to Buddhist monasticism. The lessons from the Christ are a bit extreme when viewed literally, but so are some of the examples from the Buddhist sutras. It stands as a simple view of a universal truth:

The Christ:

John the Baptist—The axe is positioned at the root of the trees. Any tree not producing good fruits will be chopped down and eliminated. [Matthew 3:10, Luke 3:9]

Better to cut off a hand then to have a hand that leads you astray. Better to cut off a foot then to have a foot that leads you astray. Better to cut out an eye then to have an eye that leads you astray. Better to enter the Dharma at all cost. [Mark 9:43-48]

The Buddha:

Abandon the defilements that keep you coming back, that give you only trouble, fruits ripening in suffering, coming back to grow old and die. Cut them off at the root, leave them as a dying stump, left behind and unable to regrow. [Nalakapana Sutta 7]

I will teach you to way that is appropriate for uprooting all conceptions. [Salayatanasamyutta 30]

Don't sell out for public approval

People will love you if you tell them what they want to hear. The truth sets you free from all of that shallow public love. The herd mentality is so wrapped up in biases and bigotries and traditions that it stands as the very antithesis of the Dharma.

Don't let anything out there distract you or discourage you. People will not understand. That is a given. They will say mean words. They will persecute you for not being like them. Know that what they don't understand is real and valuable and you will be rewarded in the end.

The Christ:

Alas for those who are spoken well of by the crowds. This is the fate of false prophets. [Luke 6:26]

Blessed are those persecuted for upholding righteousness. The Dharma is your treasure. Blessed are those abused and persecuted and disputed against because they don't understand me. You should rejoice and be glad in your reward of taking your place among the prophets. [Matthew 5:10-12]

The Buddha:

You who are overcome and obsessed with wanting to be praised will be reborn in a state of disgrace. [Labhasakkarasamyutta 10]

In an evil age there is much to fear. Demons will possess those who will curse us, combat us and belittle us. We must maintain our reverent trust in the Buddha, putting on the armor of perseverance in the preaching of this sutra. [Lotus Sutra 13]

Money is not God

Renounce wealth

The whole point of John being referred to in Luke 7:25 was that he stood against the material and externally appearing flaunt of Herod's puppet priesthood in Jerusalem. Go to the palace of Herod in Jerusalem and you will see some rich *sold out* holy men with very beautiful robes. That was not what John was about.

God, Dharma, the Way, the Christ, the Tao, the Buddha — is one choice that excludes choosing the quest for wealth and fame and power. Religion that flaunts wealth and fame and power has made its choice opposite of the choice promoted by the Christ and the Buddha.

The Christ:

What did you journey all the way out into the desert? Do you see a strong reed standing firm in the wind? Did you journey to see a man dressed in fine clothes? People are better dressed in the city palaces. [Luke 7:25]

Blessed are the poor for the Dharma belongs to you. [Luke 6:20]

He who has mastered the world and become rich should renounce the world. [Thomas 110]

It is impossible for a man to ride two horses at the same time. It is impossible to shoot an arrow from two bows at the same time. It is impossible for a worker to work for two jobs at the same time. He will come to concentrate on one and ignore the other. You cannot serve both the Dharma and the quest for wealth. [Thomas 47, Matthew 6:24]

The Buddha:

To dress richly, to collect weapons, and to indulge in sensual excess and wealth, are just invitations to the robbers. [Tao Te Ching 53]

To live with the most joy, you must possess nothing. To live on such joy is to become like a glowing god. [Dhammapada 15:4]

The buildup of wealth and position is the seed for destruction. If you have merit and fame you should abandon it. This is the Way of Heaven. [Tao Te Ching 9]

Don't value money

They give you money and tax you money. They define you by how much money you have and how much money you owe. They respect you for money, love you for money, and listen to you for money. It is important that you don't define yourself by your money or by the money you plan on making in the next few decades of selling your soul to working for money.

The Jews of the day of Jesus could understand the poison of money in a very graphic way. All of their coins were Roman with the image of Caesar on them. They represented a holy people having sold out for the lure of wealth. The Herodians ruled Jerusalem, controlling the Roman money. The Jews opposed to Roman occupation shunned the use of Roman coins, the Essenes forming an inter-village communal system of sharing and bartering.

The Christ:

Show me your money that you are asked to pay your tax with. Whose picture is on it? Whose name is on it? Pay to Caesar what belongs to Caesar. [Matthew 22:19-21]

The Buddha:

The ascetics following the Sakyan son do not accept gold and silver. They renounce jewelry and gold. They have given up the use of gold and silver. [Gamanisamyutta 10]

Don't covet

This should be listed somewhere within Matthew 5:21-30, but is missing. Telling a Jewish audience that they should not covet would not have stood out as being worth noting, with this already being half of the Ten Commandments—Do not covet your neighbor's house, or his wife, or his servants, or his ox, or his donkey, or anything else that is his. [Exodus 20:17]

The Buddha:

There is a Law teaching that you should not take anything that does not rightfully belong to yourself. I say—do not covet or even admire such an object. [Surangama Sutra]

Beware traps of wealthy elitism

Pity those who *live for wealth* and *feast and party* and think of themselves as being better than those who are poor. Envy those who

74

have collected Dharma Treasure, taking their eternal sustenance in the Dharma and celebrating in the Dharma.

The Christ:

Woe for the wealthy — your consolation is only for a short time. Woe for the feasting — you will once again be hungry. Woe for the celebrating — you will once again discover mourning and weeping. [Luke 6:24-25]

The Buddha:

If the Perfect Sage wishes to convince people to abandon their divisions, he should not set aside those considered better by praising them. [Tao Te Ching 3]

Money cannot buy eternal happiness

What determines being rich or poor in this realm of material wealth is not what ultimately is of value.

The Christ:

A rich man royally dressed and magnificently feasting every day died. A poor diseased beggar called Lazarus would lie by his gate longing for the trash to be thrown out to him. His only companions were dogs who licked his sores. The poor man died and was carried away by angels to Abraham's embrace. The rich man died and was tormented. [Luke 16:19-23]

The Buddha:

An important king that ruled over four continents died. Not possessing four things he is not freed from a bad fate. A starving beggar wearing rags that possesses four things is freed from a bad fate. The four are — confidence in the Buddha, confidence in the Dharma, confidence in the Sangha, and the practice of virtues dear to the noble ones. [Sotapattisamyutta 1]

Pleasure is not God

Fasting

Both the Christ and the Buddha faced temptation of letting food distract them from their mission. To both, fasting was a victory over being controlled by desires.

The Christ:

Jesus fasted and the Tester said to him—If you were Son of God then stones would be your loaves. [Matthew 4:3]

The Christ answered—Bread is not enough to keep human beings alive. [Luke 4:3-4]

Some demons are only cast out by prayer and fasting. [Matthew 17:21]

The Buddha:

Blessed are those who live on nothing at all. We shall feed on rapture like the streaming radiance devas (angels).

Then Mara the Evil One realized the Blessed and Fortunate One knows, and sad and disappointed he disappeared right there. [Marasamyutta 18]

Suppose I stop eating food entirely. Then deities came to me saying they will infuse heavenly food into the pores of my skin and I will live on that. [Mahasaccaka Sutta 27]

Look away

Watch what you watch. What you pay a lot of attention to becomes a chain, a weight, a disease, and a preoccupation.

The Christ:

If you look at a woman with desire, your heart has already experienced her. [Matthew 5:28]

If you find a speck in your right eye, pick it out and throw it away. [Matthew 5:29]

—Or, taking the more graphic version of the saying:

If your eyes snare you, it would be better if you ripped them out and threw them away. It is better to live blind then to be tormented with visions. [Matthew 18:9]

The Buddha:

When unwholesome states have arisen, and they
are tolerated and not abandoned, not removed,
not done away with, not annihilated, they
accumulate like flies' eggs. Not being picked out,
not being taken care of, forms seen and grasped at,
their signs and features contemplated, the eye is
left unguarded. This leaves opportunity for
growth of unwholesome states of covetousness
leading to grief. [Mahagopalaka Sutta 6-7]

Pick out the flies' eggs. When a thought of sensual
desire has arisen, do not tolerate it, abandon it,
remove it, do away with it, and annihilate it.
[Mahagopalaka Sutta 19]

A man with good eyes who doesn't want to see
what is in front of his face can either shut his eyes
or look away. [Vitakkasanthana Sutta 5]

Beware lingering desires

It is not enough to simply stay away from your addictions. If you keep
thinking about them, they still have control over you. Let them go in
your mind as well as in your hands.

The Christ:

One going out and wandering through a desert
that carries along an unclean spirit seeking a
means to fulfill its desire will never be satisfied.
He will return home. Arriving he finds it
abandoned, clean and uncluttered. The unclean
spirit makes itself at home, inviting seven other
spirits more wicked than itself, and they all make
it their home. That person ends up worse off than
before. This is the fate of this generation.
[Matthew 12:43-45]

The Buddha:

There are huge trees with tiny seeds and huge
bodies, encirclers of others trees. The trees they
encircle become bent, twisted, and split. Some
clansmen have left behind sensual pleasures and
gone forth from the householder life into
homelessness. Those same sensual pleasures or
others even worse than them cause him to become
bent, twisted, or split. [Bojjhangasamyutta 39]

DHARMA LESSON: If you wish to be complete, sell your possessions, giving it all to the poor to assure yourself of heavenly treasure. Leave it all behind to be like me. It is difficult for you who are attached to possessions to come to accompany the Dharma. It is easier for a camel to stoop to crawl through a tiny hole in a wall than for you who are attached to possessions to accompany the Dharma.
[Matthew 19:21-24, Luke 18:24-25]

Teleios is usually translated as perfect, but it means more than that in Greek. It is the setting out for a definite goal or purpose, to have an aim, and then to complete that goal. It is not a static state of a detached perfection, but rather an accomplished journey of growth. Be teleios as your Father in heaven is teleios. [Matthew 5:48]

A camel going through the eye (*trupema*, meaning aperture, opening) of a needle (*rhaphis*, meaning puncturing, as in a passageway through a wall) would have to be unpacked. The stuff on his back would have to be removed. He would have to bend down on his knees and crawl through. This was a very difficult task for a camel owner, camels being stubborn about being put through such an ordeal, and the owners being fearful of losing their possessions which they would have to then carry though to the camel on the other side. The message of the parable is that possessions define you, weight you down, and prevent you from finding the secret passage to the realms beyond the wall. What is beyond that wall through that narrow passage is a place of completion, of fulfillment, of perfection, a heaven on earth. This Pure Land of Dharma is beckoning. But your camel cannot get through until it is unpacked and ready to go. You have to unpack yourself from the curse of the desire to possess more and more stuff, of money running your life. [Mark 10:23-25] You have to unpack your camel to pass into the Dharma.

Those who have abandoned having homes, wives, siblings, parents, children—for the sake of the Dharma will be abundantly rewarded in this present aeon (realm) and reach that eternal aeon (realm) of life. [Luke 18:28-30]

To leave behind the family ties in search for enlightenment was Siddhartha Gotama's first step toward Buddhahood. It makes perfect sense within the framework of devoting your life to being a monk or nun in the Buddhist orders. The fetters and chains of supporting a spouse and children were taken out of the picture of a life devoted to awakening. The desire to be a homeowner with a spouse and children was unpacked from their camels. Everything that makes for status symbol—size of house, number of possessions, beauty of wife, strength of children—unpacked from the camel. The abundant rewards of the treasures of the Dharma are not only presently enjoyed within the context of this aeon (age), but will last for eternity.

Celibacy

DHARMA LESSON: This is not for everyone, but only for those who can accept it. There are those who have vowed to remain virgins from birth, as a human choice, for the sake of the Dharma. [Matthew 19:11-12]

Monks and nuns from the Buddhist traditions took up vows of celibacy. This tradition carried over into Christian monks and nuns and priests. The word *eunovchizo* is traditionally translated as eunuch. The term in Greek means one who selects to be unmarried and prefers to not engage in sexual activity.

Solitary holiness

Otherworldly

An overall dissatisfaction and restlessness drive the mystic into higher and higher experiences. No religious place is called home for long, no safe haven of a philosophy or structure of any type. It is truly a dark night of the soul, as St. John of the Cross noted.

The Christ:

> Foxes have their dens. Birds have their nests. The human child has nowhere to rest his head. [Matthew 8:20, Thomas 86]

The Buddha:

> Those who have higher thoughts are always reaching out, not being happy to call any place home. [Dhammapada 7:2]

> As the deer roam free without ties, the bhikkhus live homeless. [Vanasamyutta 4]

Let it go

If all you ever focus on is what your next meal will be and how you will dress for the occasion, you are living a pretty shallow useless life. The purpose of the Dharma is to wake you up to realizing that there is more to life than just getting more and more experiences that are supposed to make you happy and fulfilled, but just end up making you fat and miserable.

Dharma places you beyond the control of being defined by pains and pleasures, of your worries, of all the issues that manipulate most people just like they are puppets starring in the show of their own lives. The saying goes "let go and let God." The Dharma makes it OK for you to let it go, to stop stressing out over the little things.

Don't you want to look back on your life as having been a good fulfilling experience? The way to arrive at that point is to stop planning ahead so much and jump into each day fully living it as it is here. Then your life will have been a collection of countless wonderful fully alive days that you directly experienced. Pay attention to now. Start right now. It will begin to add up.

The Christ:

Don't focus upon tomorrow. Tomorrow will take care of itself. There is enough to pay attention to today. [Matthew 6:34]

Life is more than what you eat, what you drink, and the clothes your body wears. There is more to life than food. The body is more than clothing. [Matthew 6:25]

The Buddha:

Don't dwell on the past or live in hopes for the future. The past it is gone. The future has not yet arrived. Instead, look with insight into each presently arisen state. Know it. Be sure of it. Without thought of failure, or being shaken off course, put your effort into today. You may be dead tomorrow. No bargaining with death can hold its overwhelming arrival. But you who can live passionately and relentlessly with each present day, each present night, your death will remain a single excellent night. [Bhaddekaratta Sutta 3]

Sensual pleasures provide you with little real gratification. Instead, they bring much suffering, despair, and danger. [Alagaddupama Sutta 3]

Be moderate in eating. Be sensible. Don't eat for amusement. Don't eat until you are passed out. Don't eat food because it is something you crave. Eat for the energy required to maintain physical health, for stopping the feeling of hunger, and for fueling your holy work. [Ganakamoggallana Sutta 5]

Discontent and delight do not conquer you who fulfill the precepts. As such you will transcend the arising of your desire to control. [Akankheyya Sutta 7]

Fear and dread do not conquer you who fulfill the precepts. As such you will transcend the arising of your desire to control. [Akankheyya Sutta 8]

The requirements of life that are needed to be obtained by you who have gone forth, clothing, food, a place to rest, medicine, will be difficult to come by. These concerns did not stop me from going forth from the home life into homelessness. [Vanapattha Sutta 3-4]

Dharma Lite

No props. No laptops with projectors. No handouts. No passing out of Bibles. No television cameras. No streaming video. The Dharma is best presented without the big show. The Dharma is not a form of entertainment in a showy church service. Dharma is real, one-on-one, direct honest communication of what each of us may simply experience. Dharma is carried in the heart as an eternal potential to burst forth as needed in any given situation. It has to be passed on as such and not cheapened by media.

The Christ:

Take nothing with you but your walking stick—no food, no bag, no money. Take only the shoes on your feet and the clothes you are wearing. [Mark 6:9]

The Buddha:

Become content with only the robes you wear, trusting in alms for your food, taking nothing else with you. [Culahatthipadopama Sutta 14]

Content with the robe on your body, trusting in alms food to maintain your stomach, wherever you go, taking nothing else with you—Just as a bird, wherever it ventures, flies with only its wings to have to be carried. [Kandaraka Sutta 15]

Solitude

This example of the solitary vision quest is perhaps the greatest teaching given by both the Christ and the Buddha. Everyone needs to come to grips with what it means to be *authentic* apart from the distractions of the herd. What is right for the masses, put to a vote and agreed upon by the majority, may not be what is right for the solitary on a mystical quest. Once you discover who you truly are, then returning to the crowds you can maintain your sense of identity that eludes them.

The Christ:

Blessed are those who have experienced being solitary, for you will find the Dharma. You are its children and it is your destiny. [Thomas 49]

Sending the crowds away he went up into the hills by himself to pray. [Matthew 14:23]

Long before dawn, he rose and departed from the house and went to a deserted place to pray. [Mark 1:35]

He would retreat into a deserted place to pray. [Luke 5:16]

Jesus was engaged in solitary prayer. When he returned to his disciples he asked them who he was in relationship to humanity. [Luke 9:18]

Remain here while I go off alone to pray. [Matthew 26:36]

The Buddha:

It is not proper for me to live with a crowd like this. I must live alone, withdrawn from this crowd. [Mahapadana Sutta 2:17]

The first meditative state is accompanied by applied and sustained thought of rapture and pleasure created in a state of seclusion. This is a state higher and more sublime than knowledge and vision. [Culasaropama Sutta 13]

Resort to a secluded resting place, the woods, underneath a tree, on a secluded mountain, a ravine, a cave on the side of a hill, a graveyard, the thicket of a jungle, an open field, or a heap of straw. [Maha-Assapura Sutta 12, Kandaraka Sutta 18]

A holy man does not find his light in the crowds of people in society. [Mahasunnata Sutta 3]

Entering the forest, you gain confidence, steadiness, decision, detached from the disturbances of the village and the encountering of people there. [Culasunnata Sutta 4]

If you find no worthy friend, no virtuous steadfast companion, then as the lion king explores his conquered realm, walk in the woods alone. [Upakkilesa Sutta 6]

Defeated is the army of pleasant and agreeable contacts. Meditating alone, I discover a blissful attainment of my goal, a heart at rest. Thus I avoid closeness with people, not forming intimate ties. [Marasamyutta 25]

Without informing his closest companions, without dismissing the bhikkhu Sangha, he set out on a solitary journey without a companion. [Khandhasamyutta 81]

Cleanse your ego

Nhataka is a baptism ritual ceremony denoting completion of training for Buddhist monks. The Essene Baptist sects performed ritual baptism as an initiation rite into their holy community. It symbolizes taking a step that is forever a transformation. It is the point of no return. If you have taken this step, forces will push you along the rest of the way. This is not saying that baptism is a magic bullet that automatically causes you to arrive at the destination. Baptism is a seal, a symbol, of a force that sanctifies the person, called the *Divine Breeze*, the *Sanctified Wind*, and the *Holy Spirit* by early Christians, Wind being the same word as Spirit in Greek. The ancients considered there to be four "elements" that defined our very states of being. They are earth, water, wind, and fire. Earth is of course the physical substantial dirt of our being. To be baptized in water, or in wind, or in fire, symbolized resurrecting into higher states of being. Each stage was seen as an initiation into a level of being from which you could never again descend. This is understood by Baptist Christians as *once saved, always saved* and baptism symbolizing this salvation.

The Christ:

John the Baptist—I baptize you in water as a sign of repentance. One who comes after me is more powerful than I. He will baptize you with the Holy Wind and Fire. [Matthew 3:11, Luke 3:16]

Who has faith to the extant of being baptized is assured of salvation. [Mark 16:16]

The Buddha:

A bhikkhu has been washed who has washed off evil unwholesome states that defile. [Maha-Assapura Sutta 25]

Misunderstood

Don't expect your family or coworkers to understand your eccentric mysticism. Be ready for them to tease you or to turn against you for not being like them. Holy people have experienced this for ages and in various cultures. It comes with the territory.

The Christ:

A prophet is despised only in his own country and in his own house. [Matthew 13:57]

The Buddha:

Ratthapala the venerable holy man went to his own father's house and he received there neither alms nor polite words, but rather only abuse. [Ratthapala Sutta 17]

Transcending

Rise above the ordinary, stand apart from the herd and free yourself from identifying yourself as being one of them. In your solitary mysticism you gain an authenticity that takes you beyond the limitations of the culture's paradigm. You see from a higher plane. What matters to them is all but completely ignored by you. Truth consecrates you and protects you from the defilements and distractions of the culture. This includes the culture's religions. You no longer want their stuff, no longer care to compete, no longer care what they think of you, and no longer want their blessing.

The Christ:

I gave you the Dharma and the world hates you for it. You belong to the world no more than I belong to the world. I am not asking for you to be removed from the world, but to be protected from harmful influences (poneros). You belong to the world no more than I belong to the world because you have been consecrated in the Truth. [John 17:14-17]

The Buddha:

As a lotus flower is born in the water and grows up in the water, but having risen up above the water, it stands without a spot of the water, you are born in the world, grew up in the world, but having overcome the world, stand without a spot of the world. [Khandhasamyutta 94]

The resurrection from mortal body to transcendental body does not involve mortal death. The old body continues to live and the old mind serves its needs, but it is now freed from mortal thinking. There has occurred an inconceivable transforming death. [Lankavatara 11]

Live with an abundant and exalted state of mind, transcending the world in your firm determination. Doing so, there are no more evil unwholesome mental states. No greed. No ill will. No presumption. Abandoning these states achieve a state of mind that is unlimited, immeasurable, and well developed. [Anenjasappaya Sutta 3]

Death

Don't for a second think of any of this as lasting. It is all composed and will all decompose. As soon as our bodies stop growing up they start dying. You body will be dead soon—in a few short decades, and there is nothing you can do about it. If you trust in anything to lastingly identify as being who you are, it must be something beyond the composed changing dying shell you inhabit.

The Christ:

Can any of you in all of your concern add one instance to your lifespan? You worry about what to wear. Consider the flowers growing in the field. They never spin about with concerns, yet they are dressed in royal robes more splendid than those of Solomon. If God clothes the wild flowers growing in the field, which are there for but a day and then thrown into the fire, why can't you have enough faith to know God will look after you? [Matthew 6:27-30]

The Buddha:

A longer lifespan is not purchased by wealth. Prosperity cannot banish getting old. This life is short, the sages understand. It cannot know eternity, only change. The rich and poor alike touch their end. The fool and sage as well feel it. While the fool is stricken by folly, no sage will ever tremble at the touch of their end. Better is wisdom for this reason than amassing wealth, since wisdom is the price of the final goal. [Ratthapala Sutta 42]

Generous heart

Both the Buddha and the Christ presented the image of the poor people with giving hearts as compared to rich people who hold back on their charity. I have read that the Buddha taught about a widow who gave two coins to the monks, but I have never found the original source. It is the timeless lesson that it is not the gift but the heart that counts.

The Christ:

He sat apart from the treasury and observed
people coming with their contributions. There
were several wealthy people who gave large
sums. He observed a poor widow lady who
offered two pennies. He gathered his disciples to
teach—If the truth is told, this poor widow lady
has offered more than all of the others who
contributed today combined. They all gave their
spare change, but she is poor and has offered all
that she had to live on. [Mark 12:41-44]

The Buddha:

Some provide from the little they have. Others are
rich and hold back on their giving. An offering
given from what little you have is worth a
thousand times its actual value. [Devatasamyutta
32]

Killing the ego

The ego is strong, surrounding itself with cravings and plans to remain
in control. The mystic wants to remove the cravings for wealth,
simplify life, and stop the ego from running the show. There has to be
a coup, a changing of the guards. Once you trust yourself and see
yourself as your own friend, it is then easy to take control of your own
life.

The Christ:

How can you make your way into a strong man's
home and plunder his property? You would first
have to restrain the strong man. Only then could
the home be plundered. [Matthew 12:29]

The Buddha:

A wealthy man with riches and property,
protected by a bodyguard, was the target for a
man who wanted to take all of his wealth, damage
his home, and endanger him to the point of death.
The man considered that it wouldn't be easy to
take him by force. So he approached him as a
friend, gaining his trust. Then finding himself
alone with him, he took his life with a sharp knife.
[Khandhasamyutta 85]

It's up to you

DHARMA LESSON: Here are the keys to the Dharma —
what you hold on earth will be held in heaven, and what
you let go of on earth will be let go of in heaven. [Matthew
16:19]

When you read this as being something just for old *Pope Peter*, as some exclusive initiation rite of an institution, you miss the most important message contained in the gospels. These are the long lost top-secret symbols from the ancient amulet discovered at the bottom of the ocean. These are the Dharma keys. This is the passageway into awakening. What you bind and accept and hold in the here and now is eternally a part of who you are. What you loosen and extinguish and let go of in the here and now, you have eternally become free of. Your immediate decisions have effect on your eternal being. Your earth is your transient mundane life, your daily choices, your loves, your desires, what you put your energy into and identify yourself with. We are talking about the things that you are tuned to and resonate with. These earthly choices create a heavenly karma. Desires that occupy your daily life also hold you back at an eternal level. Desires that are let go of in your daily life also have an effect of freeing up your eternal level for greater spiritual progress. Simple key. Profound truth.

Selection

DHARMA LESSON: A net catches all fish. Keep the ones
you want and throw the rest back. [Matthew 13:47-48]

This implies that you are called to take control of your own Dharma experience. Consider all and be diligent about your own salvation. Keep what is useful to you and don't burden yourself with what is not. Such an open-minded approach was a shocking clash to a narrow-minded xenophobic fundamentalist audience. To give the individual the power of selection, of control over choice, of free will direction of spiritual destiny, was not held by those who wanted to control the spirituality of people by institutionalizing religion and defining what is to be considered to be scripture and what is the correct interpretation thereof.

Use the words of books as possible pointers to what you can directly experience. Treasure the pointers that work for you. Let go of the pointers that for now seem to not work for you. The ultimate value is not in the words but in the application and result. Orchard trees are valued because of their fruit. Words are valued if they steer you in the right direction.

Community sacredness

The Poor

DHARMA LESSON: Blessed are the breathing beggars, for they have the Dharma. [Matthew 5:3]

This sounds like a very strange translation. The word that is normally translated as poor is *ptochos*, which doesn't simply imply a lack of wealth. The word specifically means a mendicant renunciant, one who has given up on having a normal life due to the pursuit of spiritual matters, like the Therapeutae or Essenes having renounced possessions and money. The Greek culture supported its philosophers because it valued what they could think if given the freedom from the worries of leading a normal lifestyle. In the East, it was common to encounter wandering ascetics, yogis in search of higher truths, Buddhist monks with their begging bowls. The idea of being a wandering holy man prophet had a long history among the Jews, but it seemed that among the Essene communities of the day of Jesus that it was becoming much more popular of an alternative to trying to earn more coins with the image of Caesar on them. In the Dead Sea Scrolls the term *the Poor* was used to define those holy communities that shunned Roman money and the corruptions of associating with the tainted wealth of Herod's Jerusalem.

Why breathing? Matthew's version adds the word *Pneuma* into the statement, which is usually translated as "in spirit" but which literally means breathing. Breathing is an exercise in awareness in the East. For someone to have abandoned the quest for riches, to have become a wandering ascetic, and to have learned meditation techniques, the reward is the Dharma. To have added this word and to just to have meant that you have abandoned the lure of wealth in your heart without having physically given it all up seems to water down the message in a compromise that seems unbefitting Matthew's gospel. For those breathing in (inspiring) the Holy Spirit after having abandoned the attachments of this world, the Dharma is theirs. Maybe a stretch in translation, but at least it gives us something to ponder. Try reading Luke 6:20 as: Renunciants gain the Dharma. In any case, Jesus is definitely referring to something that can be gained only by giving up aspiring for other goals, a change in focus on what you value, on what you are breathing in.

6. WHERE THE DHARMA LEARNS TO TAKE FLIGHT

The next advice from the Buddha, after having talked and walked the Dharma and having aligned and prioritized your meaning in life, is for you to finally reach up into your potential and take flight. Right effort is the willful self-pushing after aligning your life. It is an offering of a living sacrifice back to God, a vibrant song, an inspired dance, and a sincere smile. Effort implies that for at least part of the journey, it is all up to you. Like hang gliding. Christ can lead you to the top of the mountain and give you a push off. Then it is you who are in flight, having been trained and prepared and equipped.

This is your vision quest of discovering the purpose of your life and what effort you need to put into it, what you need to contribute back to the world in the name of the Dharma. This sixth spoke of the Dharma Wheel rests on the foundation you have made with the previous five spokes. You began by wanting more out of religious pursuits than mindless blind faith and meaningless speculation. You lit the fire of the desire to directly experience the spiritual. You then discovered the breath of your own free will and learned how to be authentic and original. You learned how to let go. Then plunging into the sea of words, you learned golden silence and the knowledge of how words limit and impact and define people. You touched the Dharma dirt in developing meaning and charity and good intent for everyone you encountered. By this you gained a sanctified peace. Then back upstream, you learned the values of a detached life of solitude, being in the world and yet not of it, purifying your interactions with society. Now you are ready to fly solo, but know you are never alone.

Focus on yourself

Ready your life for God to work in it

Tend to the garden that is your own personal life. You will get out life what you put into it. What you plant will be what you harvest. The more weeds you can clear out of the way, the more crops you will harvest. It is just simple soul farming.

The Christ:

I am the Planter of the Seed. The Seed is the Will of God. As I sow my Seed, I notice what becomes of it. Some fell on the road and the birds came and ate it, so it never had a chance. This is like the people who are without God, and what little they receive is taken away from them. Some fell on rocky soil. The seeds sprang up quickly, but they had no root due to the rocks. This is like the people who are enthused as long as they do not have to stand the test. When the sun came out and the wind blew, there was no root to keep them alive. This is like the people who fall away from the Will of God when it means they will have to sacrifice. Some of the soil that the Seed fell on was overgrown with weeds. This is like the people who are choked with the attachments and pleasures of this life. As weeds take away from the strength the soil has for the plant, so do desires take away from the Will of God. Some of the Seed fell on well-prepared soil, and it sprang up and grew to bear fruit in plenty. This is like those who give their lives to the Will of God. Good soil is an honest and good heart, one who has heard the Word and kept it and produced fruit in patience. [Thomas 9, Matthew 13:4-23, Mark 4:3-20, Luke 8:5-15]

The Buddha:

Faith is the seed. Good works is the rain. Wisdom is the plough. Mind is the rein. The handle is the Dharma. Determination is the goad. Work is the ox. Ploughing destroys the weeds of illusion. Harvest is the fruits of Nirvana. [Kasibharadvaga Sutta 2]

A farmer went into the woods with a plough and seeds. The soil there had never been disturbed, with tree roots and rocks. The seeds were broken, rotten by exposure to the heat for a long time. The seeds were not placed very deeply into the ground. There was not much rain. Do you think the farmer's seeds will germinate, sprout and grow, giving him a large crop? [Payasi Sutta 31]

Those with shallow understanding, wrapped up in the five desires, cannot comprehend it when they hear it. Do not preach to them. Such people will fail to have faith and will slander this sutra, quickly destroying the seeds for becoming a Buddha in the world. [Lotus Sutra 3]

90

Consider a bad field with stumps not cleared. The seeds planted there would be broken, spoilt, damaged by wind and sun, unfertile, in shallow soil, and the sky could not supply them with sufficient water. There is no way those seeds will come to growth, increase, and expansion. This is the way it is when the Dharma is badly explained, badly proclaimed, unemancipating, not conductive to peace, proclaimed by one who doesn't fully understand it. This is like a bad field. [Sotapattisamyutta 25]

Ready your world for God to work in it

You have to ready your field for God to work in it, for God to sow the seeds and watch over the development of your life living up to its divine purpose. Remove the obstacles — the ruts, the bumps, and the curves. Maintain a simple level smooth uncluttered life. The Lord helps those that help themselves, as the timeless saying goes.

The Christ:

A lone voice cries in the desert — Prepare a way for the Lord. Make his paths straight. Fill in the valleys. Level the hills. Straighten the winding paths. Smooth out the bumpy roads. All humanity will get a chance to see God's salvation. [Luke 3:4-5]

The Buddha:

His realm will be decorated for his majesty, cleansed of impurities and evils, discarded trash, overgrown thorns, and disgusting waste. The land will be made smooth without hills or valleys, without pits or protrusions. [Lotus Sutra 6]

Private personal space

The answers are not out there. The answers are within. It doesn't matter what anyone else has concluded out there, what they have constructed, what they have to offer. It only matters what is heartfelt and authentic once you close the door and you are all alone. You are your own channel to the divine.

The Christ:

When you pray (prosevchomai — to earnestly want to know the result of your desire), go to a private room, close the door, and so pray to your Father in that secret place. Your Father who sees all that is secret will reward you with the answer. [Matthew 6:6]

Blessed are the solitary and elect, for you will find the Dharma. You are from it and you will return to it. [Thomas 49]

The Buddha:

Go into your room. Keep the door closed. Know the secrets of the world. Shut the window. Observe The Way of Heaven. The further you explore, the less you know. [Tao Te Ching 47]

The disciples of the Teacher who live in seclusion are failing to train in seclusion, in not abandoning what the Teacher has taught them to abandon. They care for luxuries, leading the way to backsliding, neglectful of seclusion. [Dhammadayada Sutta 6]

Purify

Throw away choking tradition and thrive

Examples of traditions that become mindlessly followed that have choked entire cultures are bigotry, slavery, discrimination, intolerance, persecution, censorship, violence, and materialism. Question every tradition that was passed on to you and get rid of the reactions and habits that are holding back your Dharma growth. Get rid of what drains you and add on what feeds you. You have to build up your Dharma strength, like a spiritual immune system.

The Christ:

A fig tree in a vineyard was without fruit for three years. A man dug around it and fertilized it, hoping it will bear fruit the following year. [Luke 13:6-9]

The Buddha:

A large tree grove was choked with weeds. It was tended by a man who cared for it. He cut down and threw out the crooked saplings throughout, cleaning the grove and tending to the straight and well-formed saplings. The grove will now come to growth, increase, and fulfillment. [Kakacupama Sutta 8]

Inner battle

The simple path gets obstructed and replaced with another that leads people away from the happiness, growth, increase, and fulfillment that was the Dharma's original destination. It is like the dreams of childhood being replaced with the concerns of adulthood. The pure crop of Dharma gets intertwined with weeds. If you are sleeping, you may not notice you are now off course, may not realize that there are now weeds in your garden, overgrown. The deer herd needs to be protected. The wheat crop needs to be protected. Your Dharma nature is the good man who opens the Way and plants the wheat. Your ego is the enemy who wants to get distracted, to let the Dharma deer die and the Dharma wheat get lost in a field of weeds.

The Dharma is like good seed planted in the heart. Weeds are the desires that haunt the heart to try to choke out the Dharma. Asceticism to destroy the weeds when the Dharma is still young could also hinder the Dharma. Gotama's first realization in awakening was to realize that he could never reach the Dharma from a state of extreme self-denial. This is when he discovered the Middle Way. No longer defined by his desires, he was at the same time, no longer defined by destroying his desires. It was enough to see clearly from a detached frame of reference, to know what was the Dharma and what were the desires. To know the grain from the weeds was enough for now. The harvest of Dharma, the maturing of spiritual development, will provide a time to collect the fruits of Dharma and to extinguish the weeds. Just being in a state of awareness is enough for the Middle Way.

The Christ:

A man planted good seed in his field. When all slept, the enemy came and planted weeds. When the wheat sprouted and ripened, the weeds appeared as well. At harvest time, the weeds will be gathered and burned while the wheat will be gathered and stored in the barn. [Matthew 13:24-30, Thomas 57]

Take the alternative route. The road that most take is dangerous and has a wide range of obstacles. Through the narrow gate is a straight road that leads safely to the destination, yet only few have discovered it is there. [Matthew 7:13-14]

The Buddha:

There was a wooded range with a low-lying marsh that was home to a large deer herd. One man desired their ruin, harm, and capture, so he closed the safe and good path that led to their happiness and opened up a replacement false path so that the deer might come upon calamity, disaster, loss. Another man desired their good, welfare, protection, so he reopened the safe and good path that led to their happiness and closed off the replacement false path, destroying the temptation. So the large herd of deer proceeded to growth, increase, and fulfillment. [Dvedhavitakka Sutta 25]

Resounding with a host of nymphs, haunted by a host of demons, this tangled forest of delusion— how do you escape from it? The straight way is the name of the path to the fearless destination. You may follow this way with the strong chariot riding on wheels made up of wholesome states. Disgust with what is wrong is its floorboard. Mindfulness is its seat. Dharma is the chariot driver. Right view is the horse. You who have found such a vehicle have the means to approach Nirvana. [Devatasamyutta 46]

Ignoble ones fall down head first into the crooked path. The path of the noble ones is smooth, even as the noble ones are smooth in the midst of the crooked. [Devaputtasamyutta 6]

What if you saw an uneven path and another even path by which to avoid it? What if you came by boat to a rough stream and another smooth waterway by which to avoid it? [Sallekha Sutta 14]

Follow the Direct Path. [Satipatthana Sutta 2]

The mind has two doorways through which it may venture. One leads to a realization of the mind's Pure Being. The other leads to the discriminations of what appears and disappears, of life and death. [Awakening of Faith, part 3, section 1]

Dharma requires work

Blind faith without actually making an effort is worthless. Faith in Jesus, praying to Jesus, calling yourself a Christian, carrying around a Bible—these do not connect you with Jesus. Joining Jesus in his Dharma means following the Way in the offering of your life as a gift to the Father in living a life according to the will of the Father. Jesus was surrounded by people wanting to follow him around, to join the train, to see what they could get out of it. He had already given them the instructions of how to meet him in his Dharma, but it required

94

their own free will gift of taking responsibility for their own resurrection.

Cults (even big name ones with large congregations) that offer a magic bullet *nothing to do but say Amen* solution are like an all you can eat diet plan, or thinking you can exercise by sitting on the sofa. They ultimately don't work. They just wasted your time and stopped you from actually doing something to make spiritual progress in your life.

Neither the Buddha nor the Christ won popularity contests in their day, perhaps too blunt and stripped down for a world devoted to being politically correct and money driven.

The Christ:

I told them plainly that no one comes to me except by *the gift* to the Father. Then many of them went away and followed no more. [John 6:66]

The Buddha:

Fools come up to make requests of me. I speak to them the Dharma, but they only think of following me around. [Satipatthanasamyutta 3]

Sixty more gave up the discipline and returned to the lower realms of being. Difficult is the path of the resurrected. [Anguttara Nikaya 7:68]

Remove the distractions

Let go of what has been bugging you. Stop letting it infect you. Stop letting it direct you and control you. Let it go. It is not worth the worry.

The Christ:

Extract the stick from your own light and then you will see clearly to help your brother extract the sawdust out of his light. [Matthew 7:5]

The Buddha:

Being stirred is a disease, a tumor, and a dart. This is why the Tathagata lives unstirred, with the dart extracted. [Salayatanasamyutta 90]

Impurities of the heart stain the life

You can't start with an old worn out mindset and add the Dharma to it. The level of right concentration comes sixth on the list. It has to rest on the foundation of having planted and harvested new fiber for being, to have woven it into a new meaning for life, to have colored it with virtues and mystical experiences. This is why *faith without works is dead.* You have to reinvent your life. Start over. Be born again. Otherwise, it won't turn out right and the Dharma will only be impurely reflected in you. Press reset.

The Christ:

You can't mend an old ripped coat by sewing on a new piece of cloth for a patch. It will just make the tear grow worse. [Mark 2:21]

The Buddha:

What if you took an old rag, ripped and stained, and dipped it into a bright color dye—blue, yellow, red, or pink. It would look improper. The color would not be uniform. When the mind starts out defiled, no happy result may be expected. The imperfections that defile the mind—covetousness, being selfish and greedy, ill will, anger, revenge, contempt, having a domineering attitude, jealousy, avarice, deceit, fraud, showy pride, presumption, conceit, arrogance, vanity, and a lack of compassion or empathy. [Vatthupama Sutta 2-3]

Activate

Not all about you

An easy observation is that anyone blowing his own whistle is not worth paying attention to. They are to be dismissed and ridiculed as being deluded into thinking they are more important. Those who selflessly give of themselves are the ones that become renown as being truly exemplary holy people.

The Christ:

Everyone that exalts himself shall be brought down. Everyone that humbles himself shall be lifted up. [Matthew 23:12, Luke 14:11, Luke 18:14]

The Buddha:

You who praise yourself will not be respected by others. You who have discovered The Way will project no ego. [Tao Te Ching 24]

Pay attention and put it into practice

Paying attention to what you hear is more important than trying to explain what you think. If you keep listening all the time, perhaps eventually you can hear the Dharma coming through. The Dharma speaks, not only through the Buddha and the Christ, but also including the most unexpected sources. Listen to your inner voices. They may be trying to tell you something.

If you don't use it you lose it. Delusion awaits in the wings, waiting for its chance to take center stage once again and Dharma exit stage right. There really is no salvation by faith alone. If you don't apply faith into the effects of transforming your life, you can completely lose touch with what the Dharma is all about.

The Christ:

Whoever has ears that can hear should listen. [Matthew 11:15, Matthew 13:9, Matthew 13:16, Mark 4:9, Mark 4:23, Mark 7:16, Mark 8:18, Luke 8:8, Luke 14:35]

If you hear the words of the Dharma, but you haven't taken them to experience, the evil one will come and take away the Dharma from the heart. [Matthew 13:19]

The Buddha:

Listen to the Dharma with eager ears. [Bhaddali Sutta 32]

Concentrate the mind on its ability to hear. Go inside the Gateway of Dharma to hear the Transcendental Sound of Essential Mind. [Surangama Sutra: Manjusri's Summation]

Open for them the gateway to immortality. Let those who can hear realize their enlightenment. [Ariyapariyesana Sutta 21]

The Dharma cannot be easily taught by one affected by delusion. Once investigated and the states based on delusion having been eradicated, he gains a respect, he gives ear and listens to the Dharma, memorizing it, examining it, reflectively accepting it, springing up zeal for it, applying his will, scrutinizing, resolutely striving, and contractually experiencing the direct realization of the ultimate truth with a vision of penetrating wisdom. [Canki Sutta 19-20]

It is ultimately all up to you to respond

No one can transform you but you. You are a being of free will. Christ can't force you. Buddha can't force you. No one else controls what drives you, your will, your words, your actions, your choices in life, and your authenticity. The Way is a path to follow that has to willfully be participated in, performed, acted upon, and selected. You can be shown the Way, but you have to *eklektos* the Way. It will cost you your life, what you think is your life. It will cause you to give up the quests that once defined you. Your choice. If you don't get yourself together, you will be eventually be blown away.

To abandon the near shore to set out for the far shore requires that a person actually resolve to select to actually make the effort of moving and to take the responsibility for taking the journey. Jesus was not saying that *few are chosen* as if the chooser is some force external to us with some absolute predestination. The chooser is the person who freely elects to respond to the calling by beginning the Dharma journey.

Having followed the advice of Dharma, there is a substance built up, a solid foundation of being authentic and real. Such an experience brings a gnosis, a direct understanding that is not shaky blind faith. No argument can convince you that you do not know what you have directly experienced.

The Christ:

Many are given the instructions, but not all elect (eklektos) to follow the instructions. [Matthew 22:14, Matthew 20:16]

It is not by calling me Lord that the Dharma is reached, but rather by the doing of the will of my heavenly Father. [Matthew 7:21]

Everyone who listens to my teaching and does as I have instructed is like a wise man that built a house on a rock foundation. Come rain, floods, and strong winds, it will not fall. It is secure on the rock foundation. Everyone who listens to my teaching and fails to do as I have instructed is like a foolish man who built a house on a sand foundation. Come rain, floods, or strong winds, it will fall and fall hard. [Matthew 7:24-28]

The Buddha:

Few are those among humanity who go beyond to the far shore. Most people merely run up and down along the bank. [Maggasamyutta 34]

Nirvana exists and the Way leading to Nirvana exists. I have come to show the Way. When I advise and instruct my disciples, some of them attain Nirvana, the ultimate goal, and others do not attain it. What can I do about that? I can only show them the Way. [Ganakamoggallana Sutta 14]

A pot without a stand is easily knocked over. A pot with a stand is difficult to knock over. The mind without a stand is easily knocked over. The mind with a stand is difficult to knock over. [Maggasamyutta 27]

A tiny piece of cotton on the ground will be blown whichever way the wind blows. A piece of iron on the ground will not shake, quake, or tremble in the wind. It has weight and is secure in its place. [Saccasamyutta 39]

You have to actually do something to create change

Words don't create change in themselves. They may inspire actions, or they may distract from taking actions. Having a lot of word games without any actions is just in the way of actually getting anything done about a situation.

The Christ:

Faith without works is dead. [James 2:17]

The Buddha:

For you with sense doors unguarded, all is done in vain. All is like the wealth a man gains in a dream. [Salayatanasamyutta 132]

Suppose a person would hurl a huge boulder into a deep pool of water. Then a crowd would assemble around it and have prayers and praises and rituals with salutations, chanting "Come up out of the water great boulder. Ascend to higher ground great boulder". What do you think, because of the prayers of this great crowd of people, with their praises and rituals with salutations, would that boulder ascend to higher ground? [Gamanisamyutta 6]

Forgiveness leads to perfection

Forgive your neighbor's wrongs and when you pray your wrongs will be forgiven. If anyone holds anger against another, how then can compassion be gained from the Lord? [Sirach 28:2-3]

Now is the first moment from here on out. Things can be left in the past, forgiven and forgotten. Holding grudges and dwelling on the past can hold you back. They can dampen your own transformation. If you can let go of the fact that other people made mistakes in the past, and move past that, you can also move past all of your own past mistakes.

You can get beyond whatever you have done in the past by getting beyond what ever other people have done in their pasts. Forgive and stop pointing fingers and throwing gossip stones. Be forgiving in such a pure state that it cleanses the forgiving person of all *that* person ever did *off the mark*. No one is perfect — realizing this leads to perfection.

It is an easy trap to get caught in once you begin a spiritual path for you to judge everyone around you for not being as advanced as your vision of what you think everyone should be. Everyone is different, at different stages of being. Not everyone shares the Dharma vision. If you only criticize, they will not open up to your Dharma. If you can overlook and forgive, you may open a channel for communicating your vision.

Perfection comes in stages, in baby steps, in finding out what you don't like in other people and then eliminating that from your own life. If it annoys you that people litter, then volunteer to help clean up. Take what your heart tells you is wrong as an invitation to do something constructive about the situation. Turn the urge to point the finger of blame to a calling to make a positive change in the world.

The Christ:

If you can learn to be forgiving, you can be forgiven. If you cannot learn to be forgiving, you cannot be forgiven. [Matthew 6:14-15]

He who is without sin (bad karma) is allowed to throw the first stone. [John 8:7]

How can you remove a small peg from the vision of your brother? Not with the large peg blocking your own vision. Use his small peg to knock out the large peg blocking your own vision. Then deal with his small peg. [Matthew 7:3-5, Luke 6:41-42, Thomas 26]

The Buddha:

There are two types of fools. One does not see a wrong as a wrong. The other does not forgive one who is sorry for a wrong. [Sakkasamyutta 24]

When the liberation of mind by love is developed and cultivated, any karma residue no longer remains. [Gamanisamyutta 8]

The faults of others are easier to see than your own. [Udanavarga 27:1]

Do not dwell on the faults of others, what they have done or have failed to do. Dwell on what you yourself have done and have failed to do. [Dhammapada 4:7]

It is easier to see the faults of others than your own. You tend to flaunt the faults of others while concealing your own faults. [Dhammapada 18:18]

The Perfect Sage after having attained perfection does not point out the imperfections in others. [Tao Te Ching 58]

A skilled carpenter might knock out and extract a coarse peg by means of a smaller peg. [Vitakkasanthana Sutta 3]

DHARMA LESSON: The king had a day of reckoning. One man who had a debt owed begged to be forgiven. The king had pity and forgave him. The man found another who had a debt to him, and refused to forgive him. [Matthew 18:23-35]

The debt of bad karma and how to balance the books is a subject that creates the need for religious explanations. Acts that are charitable can offset the debt of bad karma from acts that are selfish. People come to religions every day, feeling guilty for past wrongs, hoping to find some eternal forgiveness. In this parable, one such person comes to religion for forgiveness, performs the rituals and everything seems to be resolved. Then this person encounters another who had a karmic debt to himself, some past wrong that has not been forgiven or forgotten. His unforgiveness then created even more bad karma for himself, and completely nullified the forgiveness he obtained from his religious experience. The moral is – eternal divine forgiveness demands as personal payment the resolve to have a forgiving heart. If you are forgiving, you become forgiven. In not seeing the bad in others, there becomes not so much bad in yourself. In caring for others, you strengthen yourself. It reminds the Buddhist of the Bodhisattva Vow in which the quest for personal salvation is replaced with the quest to find salvation for everyone. There is perhaps no greater evil than in discovering spiritual progress in yourself at the expense of judging and excluding those around you.

The canceling of debts was a concept of the day. If the Unity of the people could only become freed from Roman taxes, the debts to the tax collectors, then the only issue left would be for Jews to write off debts to one another. It was the concept of the Year of Jubilee, the pushing of the reset button of life. No one owes anyone anything anymore. To stop holding a debt over someone's head was to give the gift of freedom. To have your house paid for and to be able to retire from work is a sense of freedom that many long for. To forgive the small insignificant local debts of transactions and interactions of those around us is to somehow obtain a large significant universal forgiveness of debts for ourselves as individuals and for ourselves as a collective whole. Practical sacred.

Prepare without delay

The inner voice will not only stop calling you eventually if you continue to ignore it, you may find yourself actually blocked from it. Use it or lose it. When you are young you are soft and flexible enough to make life impacting decisions and changes in direction. If you have to take care of life first and then plan on coming back to the Dharma, you may find you are too late. The window of time has once again closed for you.

The Christ:

Ten bridesmaids were to attend a wedding. Each was to hold up an oil lamp. Five were prepared and took oil for the lamps. The other five had to go shopping for oil. The five prepared bridesmaids were attending the groom in the wedding hall. The door was shut since the wedding ceremonies had begun. The five bridesmaids who had to go shopping for oil arrived, but they were too late and were not allowed to come in by the doorman. [Matthew 25:1-13]

The Buddha:

There are roots of trees and empty huts waiting on you to begin meditation. Do not delay or else you will regret it later. This is my advice to you. [Anenjasappaya Sutta 15]

Karma of respect

You have to redefine success in terms of the Dharma. Then without obstinacy and arrogance, you find yourself ruling over your world as emperor — taking control in a world surrounded by people who are nothing more than slaves to their own passions and traditions.

The Christ:

Blessed are the meek. They will rule this planet. [Matthew 5:4]

The Buddha:

Having reached the state of being tamed, they are victors in the world. The enlightened are supreme in the world. [Khandhasamyutta 76]

You who are not obstinate and arrogant, that respect those worthy of respect, rising up in their presence, offering a seat, making way, with honor, respect, reverence, and veneration, wherever reborn will be honored, respected, reverenced, and venerated. [Culakammavibhanga Sutta 16]

You who are contented are already rich. [Tao Te Ching 46]

Time will prove that the humble will be supreme, the dishonored will be justified, the empty will be filled, and the old will be rejuvenated. [Tao Te Ching 22]

The meek and defenseless conquer the proud and strong. [Tao Te Ching 36]

The meek are the conquerors of the strong. The yielding are the conquerors of the arrogant. [Tao Te Ching 78]

Charge up

Be consistent

DHARMA LESSON: Blessed are those who persist in balance through the hardships it may bring, for they have the Dharma. [Matthew 5:10]

Dikaiosune is usually translated as goodness, but it is closer to the meaning of this Greek word to translate it as equity or as remaining balanced. Balance is the art of remaining constant through fame and shame, loss and gain, joy and pain—remaining the same. This is the real power of being a martyr for who you are, willing to even die to remain balanced. This balance is one of the keys to the Dharma. If you really know, then you won't be swayed to doubt no matter how someone argues against what you know. If you are just going on blind faith, you don't have anything to stand on in order to maintain a balance. You have to have an experience that is solid, that is a foundation, a Dharma, to stand on in the face of whatever comes your way.

Dharma growth

This parable makes little sense if Dharma is a place or a Messianic Age or Kingdom in the Sky. It makes perfect Buddhist sense, however, for the Dharma sewn in the heart to yield a bountiful harvest of growth that transforms the planter's life. It makes Jewish sense if we are speaking of the *Shekinah* of God, that heartfelt presence of the divine. Dharma is a transformative development of spiritual attributes through the course of living a holy life. Your job is being a good nurturing fertile field for the Dharma to grow in.

The Christ:

The Dharma is like a man who has put his seeds on the soil. Night and day, while sleeping and awakening, the seeds sprout and grow. He doesn't understand why, but the soil gives the seed the power to produce shoots, develop ears, and create grain. Once the crop is ready he reaps the harvest that is presented to him. [Mark 4:26-29]

The Buddha:

Whatever types of seeds are planted have their growth, increase, and expansion because of the soil, established in the soil. Planted in virtue, established in virtue, a bhikkhu develops and cultivates the Noble Eightfold Path and by doing so attains growth, increase, and expansion in wholesome states. [Maggasamyutta 150]

Expect to be misunderstood

Being misunderstood just comes with the territory. People have their narrow visions, defined paradigms, sacred traditions, and ingrained prejudices. Open honest simple Dharma does not always go over well.

The Christ:

Blessed are you when people abuse you and mistreat you and speak out against you falsely because you are mine. Rejoice and be glad, for you are greatly rewarded by heaven. [Matthew 5:11-12]

The Buddha:

Those most enlightened by The Way are the most difficult to understand. Those further along on The Way are the most withdrawn. [Tao Te Ching 41]

Back to childhood

This truth is applicable to all of the spokes of the Dharma wheel. Being born again is the stage of the Eightfold Path at which you can finally recreate yourself. After aligning your attachments, your words, your actions, and your job, the incubation period is complete and you are ready to come up out of the baptismal water to be reborn as a child of the sky.

The Christ:

The truth of what I tell is that you cannot see the Dharma without being born again. [John 3:3]

The Buddha:

You who have arrived at the state in which you do no evil bodily actions, utter no evil speech, have no evil intentions, and do not make money at any evil livelihood—I describe as being like a young tender newborn lying infant. [Samanamandika Sutta 8]

Stay young and flexible

Being young and fresh and green and alive resists the forest fires of distracting passions. Being old and dried out, a fire will quickly consume you. Being old and rigid and set in your ways makes you easier to be broken. Being young and soft and flexible, you can adapt to the world around you without being permanently defined by how the world forces your shape to be.

That Jesus identified himself as green wood instead of old dry wood resonates with this parable of the Buddha.

The Christ:

If this is what is done to green wood, what will happen to the dry wood? [Luke 23:31]

The Buddha:

Could a man light on fire a dry sapless piece of wood? Anyone who has not developed and cultivated mindfulness of the body, Mara (the devil) can do as he pleases to him. [Kayagatasati Sutta 24]

The proof is in the result

Your children are what you physically create and present to the world, what you leave behind, your legacy. Your spiritual children are the good works and projects and impact on the world that you leave behind as your Dharma legacy. When you can look back at your life and list the good you have done for the world then you know you have truly lived out the Dharma.

The Christ:

Wisdom is justified by her children. [Matthew 11:19, Luke 7:35]

James—I will prove to you I have faith by showing you my good deeds. You cannot prove you have faith with no good deeds to show for it. [James 2:18]

The Buddha:

Wisdom is purified by morality, and morality is purified by wisdom. [Sonadanda Sutta 22]

You understand a state that can be known with the eye of wisdom. The purpose of wisdom is direct knowledge, full understanding, abandoning. [Mahavedalla Sutta 11-12]

7. WHERE THE DHARMA DISCOVERS ITS ENERGY SOURCE

Something has to light your fire and keep it burning, warm you and fuel you and inspire you. Like light bulbs being useless once the sun comes through the window, small concerns that used to drive you now diminish in the light of a higher purpose.

Up to this point a lot has been required to prepare to begin the journey. Lots of *making reservations* and *packing* and *gassing up the car* and *getting money out of the bank* type preparations, but now the journey begins. What the Buddha called right attentiveness is a state of mindfulness that only comes to those who have purified their lives and intensified their resolve to begin to awaken to the simple reality of how things are. It was difficult to get past the programming of the words and the obstacles, the distractions and the ambitions, to the point at which everything in life is not filtered through bigotries and traditions and plans and reactions that have no place in the Dharma. The payback is the discovery of an internal Source that is a sixth sense of how we should be at any given situation.

Holy Spirit is a realm beyond the ability of words to properly convey. It must be experienced, realized, kindled within like a holy fire. Being attentive to this fire, mindful of what it is teaching us, we can resurrect into a force that links us to eternity. We touch our very Buddha Nature, our Christ Consciousness, our oneness with an all-encompassing divine plan.

Here we encounter the Holy Spirit, holy being *ha-gnos*. Ha-gnos means consecrated, blameless, perfect, and virgin. Actually the Greek term translates into perfectly experiencing reality, being fully awakened, which reminds us of the term *Buddha*. Holy is to know fully the purity of being a spirit in union with God. Holy is power. Holy Spirit is the dynamic aspect of the Christian image of the Divine, comparable to Buddha Nature as a Buddhist image. As such, this Holy Spirit is the means of which the faithful develop and journey to their spiritual goal. If you never understand the destination (Father), never encounter the embodiment (Son), but still have stumbled onto the Way (Spirit), then you are destined to eventually contemplate both the Son and the Father. If you think you know the Father or the Son and yet miss the Way (Spirit), you are destined to be lost until you acknowledge the very means for advancement. It is worth stating that the Holy Spirit is the aspect of God that has to be actively participated in, channeled though lives, the response of a free will to the call of the divine.

> Blessed is he who meditates upon Wisdom and reasons with understanding, who considers Her ways with his mind, pondering Her secrets. [Sirach 14:20-21]

Inner teaching

Look within for the spiritual authority to follow your own heart. Don't go looking for rabbis or gurus or pastors, expecting to be fed the answers. You have to give yourself the answers from your own internal fire that you kindled and fanned. Other people's conclusions may not be right for you.

The Christ:

> The Dharma is not observed. No one will say it has appeared here or there. The Dharma is within you. [Luke 17:20-21]

> You must never allow anyone to call you Rabbi. There is one Master and we are all brothers. Call no one on earth your father. You have only one spiritual Father. Do not even allow them to call you teacher. There is one Teacher — The Anointing. The most important is the one who is willing to work as a slave. Those who think highly of themselves will fall. Those who think little of themselves will be rewarded. [Matthew 23:8-12]

The Buddha:

> Dwell with yourself as your own island. Become for yourself your own refuge, with no other refuge. Dwell with this Dharma as your island. Have it become for you your own refuge, with no other refuge. [Satipatthanasamyutta 9, Mahaparinibbana Sutta 2:26]

> Recognize no one as your spiritual father, for no one is worthy to be known as our ancestor except the Perfect Father. [Tao Te Ching 4]

Inner source

The inner spring of holy water stands as a direct contradiction to religious institutions that want to define the "holy water" in terms of their own control. Your holy water is within you, an endless supply of Dharma — of Holy Spirit.

The Christ:

Whoever drinks water from a well will become thirsty again. No one who drinks the water I offer will ever become thirsty again. The water that I offer will become an inner spring of water, welling up and lasting forever [John 14:13-14]

The Buddha:

You who have transcended your birth, lived the holy life, completed your destiny, and have no further need to return to any state of being – you are bathed with the inner bathing. [Vatthupama Sutta 18]

It is in this inner spring that you should bathe to convert yourself into a refuge for all beings. If you speak no lies and never harm living beings and never take what has not been given to you and abide in a faith that is free from greed then what need do you have of finding a holy stream—any well will be your holy water source. [Vatthupama Sutta 20]

Develop self-confidence and singleness of mind without applied and sustained thought, with rapture and pleasures born of concentration—as though there exists a lake whose waters well up from below without any streams entering it and without any rain ever falling upon it. [Maha-Assapura Sutta 16]

To discover your spiritual spring is to learn the secret of heaven and earth. In this mysterious spring, spirit is eternally present in eternal becoming. [Tao Te Ching 6]

As rain pours down in drops on a mountain top, flowing downward to fill the cracks, gullies, and creeks, filling pools, filling lakes, filling streams, flowing into rivers, filling up the great ocean—so too a noble disciple, with confirmed confidence in the Buddha, the Dharma, and the Sangha, along with the virtues dear to the noble ones, flows onwards and beyond to the destruction of the taints. [Sotapattisamyutta 38]

If you tune in the reward is there

Christ reversed the ancient yin yang concept of balance. For the real truth of the Dharma is that for those that don't get it, it will all be dismissed and ignored. For those who have had a taste of it, the Dharma will resonate within and grow and each little hint will bring about great realizations, epiphanies, paradigm shifts, awakenings.

The Christ:

Those who have will be rewarded with excess. Those who have not will be rewarded with being deprived of the little they do have. [Thomas 41, Matthew 13:12]

The Buddha:

Those content with little will be rewarded with much. Those grasping much will lose what they had. [Tao Te Ching 22]

The mighty it humbles; the lowly it exalts; the overflowing it diminishes; the lacking it supplies. [Tao Te Ching 77]

Feedback

Supernatural Revelation

Dharma is a different way of looking at the world, hearing a different song, touching a realm that is not all together there for most people, taking to heart a meditation of a force that is very great and yet transcendental and immeasurable by physical senses alone.

To see what is not shown, to hear what is not spoken, to feel what is not tangible, and to think what could not be explained, the Dharma makes its way into the heart even though it cannot be explained and logically understood.

The Christ:

I shall give you what eye has not seen, ear has not heard, hands have not touched, and what has not entered into the human heart. [Thomas 17]

The Buddha:

In regard to things unheard before, there arose in me vision, knowledge, wisdom, gnosis, and light. [Satipatthanasamyutta 31]

The other realm cannot be seen with the physical eyes. You must clarify the divine eye. [Payasi Sutta 11]

This Lotus Sutra contains attainable understandable wisdom for sentient beings. In the face of the great amount of hostility in the world, it is difficult to accept. It has not been preached before my preaching of it now. It is the secret treasure of the Buddhas. [Lotus Sutra 14]

That which eyes have not seen, ear has not heard, mind has not contemplated, senses cannot detect, and intellect cannot rationalize, can be realized in meditation. [Tao Te Ching 14]

Voices

Intuition begins with listening to the voices—directing you, warning you, selecting for you. These have been called angels, saints, ancestors, divas, gods and goddesses. The ability to hear angelic beings gives you a distinct advantage in life in being intuitive and synchronous to the way that is your destiny. The real miracle of *speaking in tongues* is you are totally quiet and everyone hears you.

The Christ:

Suddenly there was a voice from heaven saying, "This is my beloved child who has received my blessing." [Matthew 3:17]

Holy men living in Jerusalem from all around the world came together to hear words spoken in their own language. [Acts 2:5-6]

The Buddha:

You who fulfill the precepts may wish to hear the sounds of voices divine and human from near and far. [Akankheyya Sutta 15]

Knowledge of eternal nature of being

Dharma allows you to look at this lifespan as only a small dot on a continuous line of being that reaches into the infinite past and into the infinite future. It is an understanding that has to be experienced.

The Christ:

Father Abraham rejoiced to see my Light. He saw it and was glad. I tell you the truth – I lived before Abraham was ever born. [John 8:56-58]

The Buddha:

You who fulfill the precepts may wish to recollect manifold past lives. [Akankheyya Sutta 17]

Ever since the long distant past, I have been teaching and converting the many. [Lotus Sutra 15]

DHARMA LESSON: Jesus said that there are those standing around him, hearing his words, looking at his face, which will not die until they see the Dharma display itself with miraculous abundance. [Mark 9:1]

Seeing the Dharma must be done before you face the death of the body. [Luke 9:11] *Dunamis* is the Greek word usually translated as power. It means miraculous ability and abundance. The miraculous abundance is a magical force of transforming energy. It is as if Jesus was saying, try this prescription and you are guaranteed to see results in this lifetime. No long-term heaven that only manifests itself after you are dead. You will begin to see the amazing effects. The Dharma will reveal itself in your life with results that you can define. When seen in this light, we understand that Jesus was not referring to a coming Messianic Age, not a Second Coming of himself, not a Jerusalem renewed, not a Jesus enthroned, but the Holy Spirit working miracles in the lives of people, the Dharma making a difference in the world. Actually, any other interpretation of this verse and we make Jesus a liar. This hits home the true meaning of Kingdom without any remaining doubts.

Resurrecting

Dry cleaning

Go into your inner space and continuously dry clean yourself.

The Christ:

John the Baptist—I have baptized you with water. He will baptize you with pure spirit (wind). [Mark 1:8]

The Buddha:

Sangarava—Whatever evil deed I have done during the day I wash away by bathing at dusk. Whatever evil deed I have done during the night I wash away by bathing at dawn.

The Buddha answered—The Dharma is a lake with fords of virtue, a peaceful lake the good recommend to the good. Where the masters of knowledge go to wash, they come out at the far shore with dry limbs. [Brahmanasamyutta 21]

There is too much concern for external baths. What is needed is the internal bath—which is confidence in the Blessed One. [Sotapattisamyutta 30]

Rise to the top

Resurrection as a term should mean to rise up above and beyond the mundane life to a level of distinction that is elevated due to spiritual perfection. It never seems to mean *physical resurrection* in the teachings of Jesus or the Gnostics. The transformation from death into life is a spiritual change that is made while we are still physically living. The *Treatise on the Resurrection* in the *Nag Hammadi Library* summarizes the term as the ancient Gnostics used it.

The Christ:

In all truth I tell you, whoever receives my instructions and discovers the One that is my homeland has found this eternal life. Without being brought to a judgment, such a person has resurrected from death into life. [John 5:24]

The Buddha:

When a person's mind has been fortified over a long period of time with the nutriments of faith, virtue, learning, generosity, and wisdom—that mind goes upwards toward distinction. It is as if a man submerged a pot of oil into a deep pool of water and then breaks it. All of the shards and fragments of the pot will sink down, but the oil will rise to the top. [Sotapattisamyutta 21]

Beyond distinction

The Dharma is like workers in a vineyard. Some take all day. Some take an hour. Some have built up for a long time. Some stumble into it at the last minute. All are rewarded with the same result.

The reward, the awakening, transcends karma, overwrites the effort put into it. It can come in a flash to those who have just begun. No more prestige to the chosen ones who have been in the vineyard for generations. For Siddhartha, this was the Brahmin caste. For Jesus, this was the Jerusalem priesthood. The last will be the first in the Dharma. The first will be the last to get it. Notice that it wasn't being in the vineyard for all day that was being put down, it was the feeling of superiority of those who felt like they should have preferential treatment.

The Christ:

The Dharma is like a landowner going out at dawn to hire workers for his vineyard. Going out mid-morning, he hired more workers. Going out at noon and again at mid-afternoon he did the same. An hour before dark he hired more workers. In the evening he paid them all the same. [Matthew 20:1-16]

The Buddha:

I see no difference between a disciple who has just attained liberation in mind and a bhikkhu who has been liberated in mind for a hundred years. One's liberation is the same as that of the other. [Sotapattisamyutta 54]

DHARMA LESSON: You will come to regret the day when Abraham, Isaac and Jacob, and all the Prophets come to the Dharma and you are excluded. People from East, from West, from North, and from South will gather to feast upon the Dharma. [Luke 13:28-29]

Jesus links this Dharma with the founding Fathers of Jewish faith, of a faith predating the Law, of a faith carried on by the Prophets. It is then linked to being a universal *Mahayana* scale Truth that unites the world as one. This perhaps comes as an answer to those who said that Jesus is presenting a newly made up way of thinking that opposes the traditions and the Law of Moses. The answer is that this Dharma is both timeless and universal, going back to the earliest seekers for the holy and forward to a world that resonates with the Dharma from every culture and perspective. The point was made that everyone who sincerely seeks the holy has come and will come to the same Source, the one Dharma.

8. WHERE THE DHARMA REACHES NIRVANA

Nirvana is extinguishing. Concentration is extinguishing distractions. Awareness is extinguishing ignorance, which is extinguishing ignoring. Put out the fires. Extinguish the ambitions. Extinguish having to judge everything. Extinguish the need to control. Extinguish reaction. Extinguish counting the quantities. Right concentration is the last of the eight spokes to the Dharma wheel. As wheels are circular, it may be noted that when you get to the end you go back to the beginning. With each pass around the circle, each turning of the wheel, you become purer and more perfect. The wheel needs all eight spokes to hold together, none really being more important than another. And yet, we stand at the level of concentrating upon mindfulness, of channeling the Holy Spirit. Now we are not running on blind faith in promises of hoping that we will reach a destination someday. In this concentration of awareness, it is realized that we have been there all along. It is gnosis. It is known because we have experienced it. Drop the mask and look in the mirror.

Interbeing Bodhisattva

See value in everyone

From the lofty perspective of right concentration, all seem to belong to one continuous interbeing. No more dividing the world into them and us. No more judging. No more bigotry. Everyone is the same through these rose colored glasses. All are potential Buddhas. Everyone is seen as being on the same journey on different stages, all with the same origin and destination. At any stage we observe another being currently in, we can rest assured that we have been there ourselves at some stage in our past. Bodhisattva vow makes no distinction—its lofty goal is to liberate all, everyone, without exception.

The Christ:

The sun shines on the bad as well as on the good. The rain falls on the righteous as well as on the wicked. [Matthew 5:45]

The Buddha:

The massive clouds pour rain on all, both the great and the small. The sunlight and moonlight shine upon the entire world, upon the good and the evil, upon the valued and the worthless. [Lotus Sutra 5]

I appear in the world like a large cloud that rains upon all of the dry withered sentient beings. This is so they can escape suffering, attain the joy of peace and assurance with the joys of this world and the joys of nirvana...At all times and for all beings I preach the Dharma the same way, as I would for any person...I offer a satisfied completion to the world, as the rain spreads moisture all around, to the great and the low, to the good and the evil, to the wise and the stupid. [Lotus Sutra 5]

He treats the good with fairness. He treats the bad with fairness. He treats the faithful with faith. He treats the faithless with faith. He regards them all as his children. [Tao Te Ching 49]

As there is no favoritism in the abundance of the earth, life being given to humans just as is given to dogs or trees, so you should treat all as having equal value. [Tao Te Ching 5]

Feel globally

Love globally. The Son is for everyone. Christ is for all. The Buddha is universal. Everyone has the potential and the right to receive the Dharma, without exclusion, without distinction, without reservation — everyone.

The Christ:

God loves this planet, so he gave his only begotten Son so that everyone who accepts him may not perish but may have eternal life. [John 3:16]

The Buddha:

As a mother protects her child at the stake of her own life, you must develop a generous heart for all others. Allow your state of generous love to spread about to the entire globe. [Metta Sutta 7]

Enlighten the world

Wisdom concealed is as useless as lost treasure. Better that you conceal your folly than your wisdom. [Sirach 20:30-31, Sirach 41:14-15]

You are the light for this generation. It is up to you. You have been given a light to shine into the world. It is your responsibility. There is no one else that can be *you* in the world. You are it. You are *you*.

Enlightenment comes with a responsibility. Transformation into a radiant being of light demands that you begin by shining on those around you. You are called to lighten the way for those who are seeking, to open the door for those who are knocking, and to explain the Dharma to those who are asking on whatever terms they are ready to receive it. You are called to represent Christ in your world. You are called to represent Buddha in your world. You are called to *doxazo* your heavenly Father by so doing. *Doxazo* is to dignify with an illuminating flattering focus.

The Christ:

You are the light for the planet. A city on top of a mountain cannot be hidden. A burning lamp is not placed underneath furniture. The lamp is put upon a stand to shine on everyone surrounding it. Shine your light for people to see. When they observe your brightness, they may come to illuminate (doxazo) your heavenly Father. [Matthew 5:14 & Matthew 5:16]

The Buddha:

Suppose an oil lamp burning with pure oil and a pure wick burned very brightly. So too a bhikkhu abides resolved upon and pervading a pure radiance. [Anuruddha Sutta 16]

I turn upright that which has been knocked down, revealing the hidden, showing the Way to those who were lost, holding a lamp in the darkness so those who had eyes to see could then see. [Vatthupama Sutta 21, Mahavacchagotta Sutta 15]

Give up on tending to fire made of wood. Kindle the inner light, concentrated, eternally blazing, composed of mind. [Brahmanasamyutta 9]

When the wise man is surrounded by fools, they do not recognize his wisdom if he does not speak. He should speak and explain the Dharma. He should wave his flag high. Well-spoken words are his flag. The Dharma is the flag of those who see. [Bhikkhusamyutta 7]

With a mind that is open and unenveloped, develop a mind imbued with light. [Iddhipadasamyutta 20]

After the One Thus Come has passed into extinction, the person who knows the sutras preached by the Buddha, their meaning and relevance and order, preaching them in truth according to the principles received — this person will be a light passing through the world, erasing the darkness, leading countless bodhisattvas (saints) to take refuge in the single Way. [Lotus Sutra 21]

Contact

Contact the eternal

If you want to contact the Father, enter Nirvana, meet Christ, meet Buddha, the Way is through the Dharma. Even if Jesus or Siddhartha Gotama were to simultaneously physically reappear in the world, running up to them and clinging to their bodies would not be of benefit. Living a Dharma oriented life is meeting Jesus and Siddhartha Gotama and all of the holy enlightened people who ever ventured down the same Dharma Way.

The Christ:

Anyone who has seen me has seen the Father. So how could you ask me to show the Father to you? Do you not realize that I am in the Father and the Father is in me? [John 14:9]

You believe because you have seen me. Blessed are those who have not seen me and yet believe. [John 20:29]

The Buddha:

Why do you want to see my foul body? You who see the Dharma see me. You who see me see the Dharma. [Khandhasamyutta 87]

Going home

There's no place like home. Knowing we eternally belong, and not even the death of body can take that away from us, is comforting. Nirvana (extinction) of everything that we added on to ourselves since we left home allows us to go back through the portal into the Father's presence. Shaking off the dreams we thought were real, we awaken to discover we have been home all along.

The Christ:

You expose the origin when you seek the destiny. The destiny will be where the origin lies. Blessed are you who rest in the place of origin. You will have knowledge of the destiny and will no longer fear death. [Thomas 18]

The Buddha:

All continuously are seen and unseen. The destiny is the state of origin. The state of origin is eternal. Understanding this truth of the eternal nature of all causes you to be merciful. Mercy gives way to impartiality. Impartiality is a noble state, linking you to heaven. Know that no one ever dies, even as their bodies decay. [Tao Te Ching 16]

Union with God

Brahma is the name of the one supreme God from the Hindu Upanishads, the ever-present force that can be encountered and experienced, that works through all of the other manifestations of the divine. Gotama didn't focus his message on the goal being to attain a union with God, his interest being the simple stripped down quest for spiritual progress and enlightenment. It was quickly noted that following his Way led to the same experience that the Upanishads spoke of, the oneness with Brahma. The two religions seemed to reach the same destination. What is fascinating is that the Jewish God was called the "God of Abraham", which is linguistically close to saying the "God Brahma". The concept is much the same – that of one supreme God that works through lesser divine beings, in Judaism called angels. If Gotama's Way resonated so well with bringing the Hindus of his day closer to their Brahma, it is not a far stretch to consider that this same Dharma Way could bring the Jews of the day of Jesus closer to the God of Abraham. In fact, there are many modern Jews who have incorporated Buddhist meditation into their paths and have found that it augments their own Jewish religion. What Buddha offers is a transparent overlay that can enhance any religious path. We have grown, in the West, to think that religions are mutually exclusive and fighting crusades against each other. In the East, this is not the case. No one ever fought a war for Dharma. Dharma doesn't force people to abandon their paths. It just lightens the way so that better choices may be made. The Dharma of Jesus was not to rip away from the God of Abraham, but was rather to expose a Way to union with the ancient vision of God.

The Christ:

May all be one. Father, may they be one in us as you are in me and I am in you. [John 17:21]

The Buddha:

The ascetic Gotama teaches The Way to union with Brahma. [Tevijja Sutta 39]

Respect something great

When you encounter groups or charities or causes or movements that exemplify the values of the Dharma, supporting them is like making a deposit into your eternal account. It plugs you into something greater, the Christ Consciousness, the Buddha Nature, the Holy Spirit, the Shekinah, of the world.

The Christ:

Anyone who welcomes you welcomes me and the Source of my being. [Matthew 10:40]

The Buddha:

The Sangha of the Blessed One's disciples is worthy of gifts, of hospitality, of offerings, of greetings of reverence — for they are the unsurpassed force of merit for the world. [Vatthupama Sutta 7]

Immortality

No end to Dharma teaching

The spirit of Christ lives on. The spirit of Buddha lives on. The brief lifetimes of these divine men centuries ago were but tiny windows into the eternal nature of such enlightened and anointed and awakened spirit beings. Once arrived at the state of being the begotten child of the Father, the awakened light for the world, there is no way that such beings could cease to bless and inspire the world.

The Christ:

I am with you forever, to the far reaches of time. [Matthew 28:20]

The Buddha:

At that time tell the sentient beings that I am here forever. I never become extinguished. Because of the necessity of an expedient means, at times I appear to be extinct, and at other times not. Know that as long as there are sentient beings in the many lands who are reverent and sincere in their desire to know, that I will be among them preaching the ultimate Dharma. [Lotus Sutra 16]

Metaphysical immortality

We are eternal beings experiencing temporary bodies.

The Christ:

It is spirit that can possess Life. The flesh cannot hold on. The words I have spoken are spirit and Life. [John 6:63]

He who endures to the end will be preserved (sozo). [Matthew 10:22]

The Buddha:

Sprit transcends mortality. [Tao Te Ching 50]

Take a stand on perseverance, with a gentle compliance, and with a non-violent disalarming mind. [Lotus Sutra 14]

Perfection

Born again

The Dharma causes you to be reborn into a new life with a higher purpose, loftier values, an eternal and universal perspective, unconditional compassion, and a truth that is beyond blind faith, beyond doubt, beyond being shaken by whatever comes along or by whatever happens.

The Christ:

He gave them power to be born of God, not born of blood or the flesh or because of the desire of man, but actually born of God. [John 1:12-13]

The Buddha:

You are my children, born of Dharma, created by Dharma, born of the Spirit and not of the flesh. [Itivuttaka 4:1]

Dharma desert

Dharma runs in cycles. It appears in pure form, and then it is institutionalized and defined, confined to structures and rituals that do not understand it. The dark ages came where those who claim to stand for Christ partake in torturous inquisitions, witch-hunts, violent crusades, invasions, persecutions, forced conversions. The Dharma is a living force, however, and it always returns in some form or another. In some reformer's vision it is forever present. It changes with each age because it is a living and evolving force.

The Christ:

The Light will soon no longer be in your presence.
Find your Way while you have the Light before
Darkness comes to claim you. No one walking in
the Darkness will find the Way. While you still
have the Light, partake of the Light, and be born
of the Light. [John 12:35-36]

The Buddha:

And afterward he will enter Nirvana, like the
ending of the smoke after a lamp has been
extinguished. In that evil age to follow, one who
preaches this ultimate Dharma will be truly
blessed. [Lotus Sutra 14]

Those who have become are fading away and the
true Dharma is vanishing. [Bhaddali Sutta 30]

Perfect attaining

God demands perfection. Perfection is the Way to God. No wonder
the Dharma made its home in Judaism.

The Christ:

Be completely perfect (teleios) as your heavenly
Father is completely perfect. [Matthew 5:48]

The Buddha:

A mind well concentrated, clear and blemish free,
loving towards all sentient beings—this is the way
for attaining Brahma (God). [Salayatanasamyutta
132]

Direct discovery

Dharma is directly experienced, realized and discovered by anyone
who follows the Way. You are not given creeds to believe in and blind
faith to hope for some distant salvation in the sky. You are given the
means to resurrect the very purpose and destiny of your being and to
know that you have attained your goal.

The Christ:

When you come to know yourselves, then you will
become knowing—you will come to the
realization that you are the children of the Father
of life. [Thomas 3]

If you discover what you have within you—this will save you. If you fail to discover what you have within you—you will die. [Thomas 70]

The Buddha:

The Dharma that you enter into and make into your home is realized for yourself with direct experience. [Ariyapariyesana Sutta 16]

Perfected Unity

Buddha never wanted to be the one and only. His goal is for everyone to join him in his Buddha nature. What may come as a shock to Christians is that Christ never wanted to be the one and only begotten son of the Father. He wanted to share this unity with God to everyone who could possibly experience it. He wanted to share with all of us how to be begotten of the Father—how to be *born again.*

The Christ:

I have given them the glory you gave to me that they might share the oneness of our oneness, with me interpenetrating them and you interpenetrating me. May they be so perfected in our unity. [John 17:22-23]

The Buddha:

I took my vow of hope to make all persons like me, without any distinctions to be made between us. [Lotus Sutra 2]

Beyond good and evil

Wisdom doesn't have faith. Wisdom knows. Wisdom doesn't speculate. Wisdom understands from experience. Wisdom doesn't need anything. Wisdom abandons.

God is forgiving. God is not some angry judge who is your enemy. Humanity created its own sins. Humanity can take away its own sins. Humanity created its own distractions. Humanity can abandon its own distractions. Forgive and be forgiven. Forgive yourself. Show compassion and discover compassion. It is contagious. It multiplies. Stop looking at the world through eyes that judge and condemn. The Dharma's compassion is unconditional love.

The Christ:

Take comfort, my child, your sins are forgiven. [Matthew 9:2]

The child of humanity has the ability to take away the sins of the world. [Matthew 9:6]

Show compassion and the Father will be compassionate to you. Do not judge and you will not be judged. Do not condemn and you will not be condemned. Forgive and you will be forgiven. [Luke 6:36-37]

John—We have directly understood for ourselves and have placed our faith in the love that God has shared with us. God is love, and whoever partakes of love partakes of God and God is with him. [1 John 4:16]

The Buddha:

The enlightened one is full of compassion for all beings. For him there are no transgressions. For him there is no going astray. He is not lost in the confusion, but is wise and ever mindful. For if one does not forgive those who confess transgression, harboring anger, intending judgment, strongly establishing an enmity—this is a very undelightful state to be in. Thus I forgive your transgressions. [Devatasamyutta 35]

Eternal mansions

You are not in it alone. There are higher forces pulling you in, transforming you, awaiting on you to awaken, putting you home. Home is nice. Welcome home.

The Christ:

In my Father's house there are many mansions. I am going now. To prepare a place for you I must go. When this place is prepared I will return to take you to myself so that you may exist with me. [John 14:2-3]

You have found the Path that leads there. [John 14:4]

The Buddha:

On the dissolution of the body, the holy person will reappear in a happy destination, in the heavenly world, experiencing extremely pleasant feelings, as a man on a path directed to a mansion with lofty finished rooms and comfortable furnishings. [Mahasihanada Sutta 41]

In the heart of the sea there are mansions that last for aeons — sapphires shining with a fiery gleaming clear translucent luster where iridescent sea nymphs dance in beautiful intricate patterns. [Maratajjaniya Sutta 25]

When I have attained supreme perfect awakening, in the place where I will be, I will engage the powers of transcending wisdom to draw you to myself and cause you to remain within my Dharma. [Lotus Sutra 14]

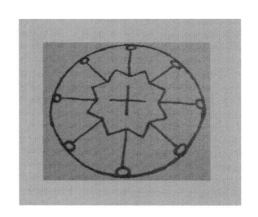

EASTERN SUTRA LIST

A lot of these can be searched for and downloaded on the Internet. All of these have been published in book form in English, though some of the books are difficult to find.

Acchariya-Abbhuta Sutta – Majjhima Nikaya 123 – Sutta Pitaka – Ti Pitaka

Aggi Vacchagotta Sutta – Majjhima Nikaya 72 – Sutta Pitaka – Ti Pitaka

Alagaddupama Sutta – Majjhima Nikaya 22 – Sutta Pitaka – Ti Pitaka

Anangana Sutta – Majjhima Nikaya 5 – Sutta Pitaka – Ti Pitaka

Anenjasappaya Sutta – Majjhima Nikaya 106 – Sutta Pitaka – Ti Pitaka

Angulimala Sutta – Majjhima Nikaya 86 – Sutta Pitaka – Ti Pitaka

Anguttara Nikaya – Sutta Pitaka – Ti Pitaka: Numbered Discourses of the Buddha from the Pali Canon of Theravada Buddhism

Anuruddha Sutta – Majjhima Nikaya 127 – Sutta Pitaka – Ti Pitaka

Akankheyya Sutta – Majjhima Nikaya 6 – Sutta Pitaka – Ti Pitaka

Ariyapariyesana Sutta – Majjhima Nikaya 26 – Sutta Pitaka – Ti Pitaka

Awakening of Faith – Mahayana-Sraddhotpada Shastra – Asvaghosha

Bhaddali Sutta – Majjhima Nikaya 65 – Sutta Pitaka – Ti Pitaka

Bhaddekaratta Sutta – Majjhima Nikaya 131 – Sutta Pitaka – Ti Pitaka

Bhikkhusamyutta – Samyutta Nikaya 21 – Sutta Pitaka – Ti Pitaka

Bojjhangasamyutta – Samyutta Nikaya 46 – Sutta Pitaka – Ti Pitaka

Brahmanasamyutta – Samyutta Nikaya 7 – Sutta Pitaka – Ti Pitaka

Cakkavatti-Sihanada Sutta – Digha Nikaya – Sutta Pitaka – Ti Pitaka

Canki Sutta – Majjhima Nikaya 95 – Sutta Pitaka – Ti Pitaka

Cittasamyutta – Samyutta Nikaya 41 – Sutta Pitaka – Ti Pitaka

Culagopalaka Sutta – Majjhima Nikaya 34 – Sutta Pitaka – Ti Pitaka

Culagosinga Sutta – Majjhima Nikaya 31 – Sutta Pitaka – Ti Pitaka

Culahatthipadopama Sutta – Majjhima Nikaya 27 – Sutta Pitaka – Ti Pitaka

Culakammavibhanga Sutta – Majjhima Nikaya 135 – Sutta Pitaka – Ti Pitaka

Culasaccaka Sutta – Majjhima Nikaya 35 – Sutta Pitaka – Ti Pitaka

Culasaropama Sutta – Majjhima Nikaya 30 – Sutta Pitaka – Ti Pitaka

Culasunnata Sutta – Majjhima Nikaya 121 – Sutta Pitaka – Ti Pitaka

Cullavagga – Vinaya Pitaka – Ti Pitaka

Devaputtasamyutta – Samyutta Nikaya 2 – Sutta Pitaka – Ti Pitaka

Devatasamyutta – Samyutta Nikaya 1 – Sutta Pitaka – Ti Pitaka

Dhammadayada Sutta – Majjhima Nikaya 3 – Sutta Pitaka – Ti Pitaka

Dhammapada – Khuddaka Nikaya – Sutta Pitaka – Ti Pitaka

Diamond Sutra – Mahayana Buddhist

Digha Nikaya – Sutta Pitaka – Ti Pitaka: Long Discourses of the Buddha from the Pali Canon of Theravada Buddhism

Dvedhavitakka Sutta – Majjhima Nikaya 19 – Sutta Pitaka – Ti Pitaka

Gamanisamyutta – Samyutta Nikaya 42 – Sutta Pitaka – Ti Pitaka

Ganakamoggallana Sutta – Majjhima Nikaya 107 – Sutta Pitaka – Ti Pitaka

Gandhari Dhammapada: Dhammapada in Gandhari language

Iddhipadasamyutta – Samyutta Nikaya 51 – Sutta Pitaka – Ti Pitaka

Itivuttaka – Khuddaka Nikaya – Sutta Pitaka – Ti Pitaka

Kakacupama Sutta – Majjhima Nikaya 21 – Sutta Pitaka – Ti Pitaka

Kandaraka Sutta – Majjhima Nikaya 51 – Sutta Pitaka – Ti Pitaka

Kasibharadvaga Sutta – Sutta Nipata 4 – Khuddaka Nikaya – Sutta Pitaka – Ti Pitaka

Kayagatasati Sutta – Majjhima Nikaya 119 – Sutta Pitaka – Ti Pitaka

Kevaddha Sutta – Digha Nikaya – Sutta Pitaka – Ti Pitaka

Khandhasamyutta – Samyutta Nikaya 22 – Sutta Pitaka – Ti Pitaka

Khuddakapatha – Khuddaka Nikaya – Sutta Pitaka – Ti Pitaka

Kosalasamyutta – Samyutta Nikaya 3 – Sutta Pitaka – Ti Pitaka

Labhasakkarasamyutta – Samyutta Nikaya 17 – Sutta Pitaka – Ti Pitaka

Lalitavistra Sutra – Mahayana Buddhist

Lankavatara Sutra – Bodhidharma

Lotus Sutra – Sadharmapundarika Sutra – Mahayana Buddhist

Magandiya Sutta – Majjhima Nikaya 75 – Sutta Pitaka – Ti Pitaka

Maggasamyutta – Samyutta Nikaya 45 – Sutta Pitaka – Ti Pitaka

Maha-Assapura Sutta – Majjhima Nikaya 39 – Sutta Pitaka – Ti Pitaka

Mahadukkhakklandha Sutta – Majjhima Nikaya 13 – Sutta Pitaka – Ti Pitaka

Mahagopalaka Sutta – Majjhima Nikaya 33 – Sutta Pitaka – Ti Pitaka

Mahapadana Sutta – Digha Nikaya – Sutta Pitaka – Ti Pitaka

Mahaparinibbana Sutta – Digha Nikaya – Sutta Pitaka – Ti Pitaka

Mahasaccaka Sutta – Majjhima Nikaya 36 – Sutta Pitaka – Ti Pitaka

Mahasihanada Sutta – Majjhima Nikaya 12 – Sutta Pitaka – Ti Pitaka

Mahasakuludayi Sutta – Majjhima Nikaya 77 – Sutta Pitaka – Ti Pitaka

Mahasunnata Sutta – Majjhima Nikaya 122 – Sutta Pitaka – Ti Pitaka

Mahavacchagotta Sutta – Majjhima Nikaya 73 – Sutta Pitaka – Ti Pitaka

Mahavagga – Vinaya Pitaka – Ti Pitaka

Mahavedalla Sutta – Majjhima Nikaya 43 – Sutta Pitaka – Ti Pitaka

Majjhima Nikaya – Sutta Pitaka – Ti Pitaka (Middle Length Discourses of the Buddha from the Pali Canon of Theravada Buddhism)

Marasamyutta – Samyutta Nikaya 4 – Sutta Pitaka – Ti Pitaka

Maratajjaniya Sutta – Majjhima Nikaya 50 – Sutta Pitaka – Ti Pitaka

Metta Sutta – Sutta Nipata 8 – Khuddaka Nikaya – Sutta Pitaka – Ti Pitaka

Nalakapana Sutta – Majjhima Nikaya 68 – Sutta Pitaka – Ti Pitaka

Payasi Sutta – Digha Nikaya – Sutta Pitaka – Ti Pitaka

Potaliya Sutta – Majjhima Nikaya 54 – Sutta Pitaka – Ti Pitaka

Rathavinita Sutta – Majjhima Nikaya 24 – Sutta Pitaka – Ti Pitaka

Ratthapala Sutta – Majjhima Nikaya 83 – Sutta Pitaka – Ti Pitaka

Saccasamyutta – Samyutta Nikaya 56 – Sutta Pitaka – Ti Pitaka

Sakkasamyutta – Samyutta Nikaya 11 – Sutta Pitaka – Ti Pitaka

Salayatanasamyutta – Samyutta Nikaya 35 – Sutta Pitaka – Ti Pitaka

Sallekha Sutta – Majjhima Nikaya 8 – Sutta Pitaka – Ti Pitaka

Samanamandika Sutta – Majjhima Nikaya 78 – Sutta Pitaka – Ti Pitaka

Samyutta Nikaya – Sutta Pitaka – Ti Pitaka (Grouped Discourses of the Buddha from the Pali Canon of Theravada Buddhism)

Satipatthana Sutta – Majjhima Nikaya 10 – Sutta Pitaka – Ti Pitaka

Satipatthanasamyutta – Samyutta Nikaya 47 – Sutta Pitaka – Ti Pitaka

Sela Sutta – Majjhima Nikaya 92 – Sutta Pitaka – Ti Pitaka

Sonadanda Sutta – Digha Nikaya – Sutta Pitaka – Ti Pitaka

Sotapattisamyutta – Samyutta Nikaya 55 – Sutta Pitaka – Ti Pitaka

Surangama Sutra: Mahayana Buddhist

Sutta Nipata – Khuddaka Nikaya – Sutta Pitaka – Ti Pitaka

Sutta Pitaka – Ti Pitaka: Discourses attributed to the Buddha of the Pali Canon

Tao Te Ching – Lao Tsu

Tevijja Sutta – Digha Nikaya – Sutta Pitaka – Ti Pitaka

Tevijjavacchagotta Sutta – Majjhima Nikaya 71 – Sutta Pitaka – Ti Pitaka

Ti Pitaka: The Pali Canon of Theravada Buddhism, completed in 246 BC

Udanavarga – Khuddaka Nukaya – Sutta Pitaka – Ti Pitaka

Upakkilesa Sutta – Majjhima Nikaya 128 – Sutta Pitaka – Ti Pitaka

Upali Sutta – Majjhima Nikaya 56 – Sutta Pitaka – Ti Pitaka

Vanapattha Sutta – Majjhima Nikaya 17 – Sutta Pitaka – Ti Pitaka

Vanasamyutta – Samyutta Nikaya 9 – Sutta Pitaka – Ti Pitaka

Vangisasamyutta – Samyutta Nikaya 8 – Sutta Pitaka – Ti Pitaka

Vatthupama Sutta – Majjhima Nikaya 7 – Sutta Pitaka – Ti Pitaka

Vimalakirtinirdesha Sutra: Mahayana Buddhist

Vinaya Pitaka – Ti Pitaka: Monastic rules of the Pali Canon

Vitakkasanthana Sutta – Majjhima Nikaya 20 – Sutta Pitaka – Ti Pitaka

Yakkhasamyutta – Samyutta Nikaya 10 – Sutta Pitaka – Ti Pitaka

WESTERN
SCRIPTURE LIST

Acts – New Testament – Bible

Dead Sea Scrolls 1QS, Community Rule: Jewish Essene

Dead Sea Scrolls 4Q424, Proverbs: Jewish Essene

Dead Sea Scrolls 4Q525, Blessings of the Wise: Jewish Essene

Hillel: Shab31a – Talmud (Jewish writings after Bible)

Leviticus – Old Testament – Bible, Jewish Torah

Luke – New Testament – Bible: Canonical Gospel

Mark – New Testament – Bible: Canonical Gospel

Matthew – New Testament – Bible: Canonical Gospel

James – New Testament – Bible: Canonical Epistle, brother of Jesus

John – New Testament – Bible: Canonical Gospel

Philip – Nag Hammadi Library: Gnostic Gospel

Sirach – Old Testament Apocrypha / Catholic Bible, important text

Thomas – Nag Hammadi Library: Gnostic Gospel

Tobit – Old Testament Apocrypha / Catholic Bible

Thomas Ragland is a native of Tennessee.

This is his first published book. His only qualification is a deep and long term love of the Dharma.

For further information, please visit the web site:

http://www.geocities.com/gnostictom/

This site contains notes and links to find and download texts from the Internet, to find newer books to order, information on how to join a discussion group with other readers about this book, and how to contact Thomas. Included in this site will be found materials not included in this book as well as information about forthcoming books.

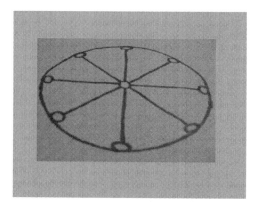

ISBN 1412000013-0

9 781412 000130

4313738

Made in the USA
Lexington, KY
13 January 2010